NUMBER 474

THE ENGLISH EXPERIENCE

ITS RECORD IN EARLY PRINTED BOOKS
PUBLISHED IN FACSIMILE

The publishers acknowledge their gratitude
to the Curators of the Bodleian Library, Oxford
for their permission to reproduce the Library's
copy, Shelfmark: 4°.C.69 Art. Seld. and to
the Syndics of Cambridge University Library for
their permission to reproduce the pages:
G3r, H4 v, I^4, K^4, L2, L3, and L4, from the
Library's copy, Shelfmark: Syn. 7.58.32

Library of Congress Catalog Card Number:
70-38209

S.T.C.No. 17823

Collation: *^{4}, A-H$^{4(-1)}$, I-L^4

JC
381
M38
1581a

Published in 1972 by

Theatrvm Orbis Terrarvm Ltd.,
O.Z.Voorburgwal 85, Amsterdam

&

Da Capo Press Inc.
-a subsidiary of Plenum Publishing Corporation-
277 West 17th Street, New York N.Y. 10011

Printed in the Netherlands

ISBN 90 221 0474 5

A BRIEFE DIS-
COVRSE OF ROYALL
MONARCHIE, AS OF THE
BEST COMMON WEALE:
VVherin the ſubiect may beholde the
Sacred Maieſtie of the Princes
moſt Royall Eſtate.

VVritten by CHARLES MERBVRY *Gentleman in
duetifull Reuerence of her Maieſties moſt
Princely Highneſſe.*

Wherunto is added by the ſame Gen. A Collection of Italian Prouerbes,
In benefite of ſuch as are ſtudious of that language.

Imprinted at London by Thomas Vautrollier
dwelling in the Blackefrieres, by Ludgate.
1581.

ALLA PRVDENTISS.ma ET
VIRTVOSISS.ma SIGNORA, LA
SERENISS.ma REINA ELISABETTA,
Reina feliciss.ma d'Inghilterra &c.

*CARLO MERBVRY humil vassallo, & minimo
seruo desidera lunga vita, & perpetua felicità.*

SI COME il viandante riguarda al Sole, il nauigante alla tramontana, & la calamita al Polo: cosi (Serenifs.ma Maestà) hauend' io à solcar con la mia debil barca nell' alto mare delle Republiche, & de gli stati; hò preso ardire d'alzar gl' occhi alla diuina, & chiara stella del suo feliciss.mo Regno; indrizzando il corso del mio viaggio, & gouernandolo tutto, secondo lo splendor, & la chiarezza di quello. Però con ogni humiltà supplico sua Sacra Maestà, che (quātunq; la mia Nauicella non habbia à pena toccate le prime spōde di quel profondo pelago) si degni pure con benigna fronte riguardarla; sgombrādo con la serenità de'i suoi reali occhi l'indegnità di quella, & del infelice nocchiere: Il quale priega diuotamente Iddio, che sua Maestà Serenissima, (Stella, Sole, Honor, & Gloria della natione Inghilese) splenda lungamente, & ci scaldi sempre con i suoi viui, & chiarissimi raggi.

TO THE READER.

I Had thought, vvhen shortly after my cōming from beyonde the Seas, I firſt entred into this boldnes of vvriting (prouoked thervnto for not looſing altogether the remembraunce of thoſe fevv ſtudies vvhich I had vſed in my late trauelles: enforced alſo by the vacantneſſe of my time (as then attending in Courte vpon her Maieſties ſeruice:) and not a litle incouraged by the vertuous and learned companie of my good friende maiſter Henry Vnton, vvith vvhome I had both in the languages and in other good letters, vvherin he is rarely indued, daily conference:) I had thought I ſaye (vvhen moued vpon theſe good occaſions I firſt tooke penne in hande) to haue onely, by calling ſome thinges to my remembraunce and by imparting them after vnto ſome fevv of my priuate Friendes, the better eſtabliſhed therby my ovvne vnderſtanding, and ſomevvhat alſo enriched and confirmed theirs: litle or nothing at all thinking that any ſuch idle exerciſes of mine should euer come vnto the open ſight, and light of the vvorlde. VVherfore calling to minde hovv I had othervvhiles beſtovved ſome time in Oxford (vnder the gouernement of my learned Tutor maiſter Doctor Humfry) in the ſtudies of humanitie: and remembring alſo hovv I had lately taken ſome litle paines in ſeeing of Cities, and Countreyes, and obſeruing their cuſtomes, and ſundry ſortes of Gouernement: I thought good to take such a kinde of enterprise in hande, as might best minister vnto me occasion to put those thinges in vse and practise, vvhich I had before time seene, and learned. Being minded therfore to reduce such my intent and purpose in Imitation of Aristotles Humane Philosophie into three seuerall partes, all tending vnto the iust consideration of a best and a most perfect common vveale (The fittest fielde me thought vvherin to runne at large my pretended courſe:) I beganne first vvith a morall treatice; vvherin after the maner of the saide Aristotle in his Ethickes, I shevved vvhat is the last Ende of a best Common vveale, applying vnto the same all such perfection of vertue, and humane felicitie, vvith all the complementes and ornamentes of externall good thinges belonging thervnto, as he did in his Moralles vnto his Summum, and ciuile bonum. A treatie, allthough not altogether to be dispised (as none such of that matter being to my knovvledge vvritten in this our English tongue:) yet because I desired not as then to bring my name in question vnto the vvorlde (hauing onely shevved such my indeuour vnto some fevv priuate friendes of mine) I laide the same a side, and proceeded vnto the seconde parte of my Institution, concerning the best forme and facion of a perfect Common vveale. VVherin, not follovving my former Guide in his bookes of Polletickes, but relying rather vpon the riper iudgement of later vvriters, and adding somevvhat also of my ovvne small experience, gathered of my late studies, and trauailes: I tooke iust occasion to preferre Monarchie aboue all other kindes of Commō vveales, and vnder the Royall mantell of the same to discouer a perfect shape of the best, and most happy state of gouernement. This Treatice both for the vvorthinesse of the matter, and for the good ende, and duetifull intent of the same,

as

as also for some other priuate causes of my ovvne: I thought good to preferre vnto a fevv honorable and vvorshipfull of my speciall Fauourers and freindes; nothing at all desiring that the same should any othervvise be seene or layed open vnto the variable speeches, and censures of the vvorld. But being further incouraged since by some, vvhose iudgement I ought not to despice, and requested also by others, vvhome I vvould be loth any thing to denie, I haue novv taken this boldnesse to publish, and impart it vnto my Countrie: hoping, that though the handling therof be but rude, and simple, yet forasmuch as the matter tendeth vnto the honour, and duetifull reuerence of our most gracious Maistriſſe (her Maiesties Highneſſe) you vvilbe as vvell contēt to reade it, as I am vvilling to recommend it vnto you. I haue added also for the benefit of such young gentlemen, as are studious of th'Italian tongue, a Collection of Prouerbes, and sentences, the vvhich I gathered in diuers places of Italie, and out of sondry approued authors: some parte vvherof also I borrovved of my freinde maister Henry Vnton; vnto vvhome, if you reape any commoditie therof, I praye you, that vvhat thankes you vvould bestovv vpon me, you vvill imparte them vnto him. Fare you vvell.

✽ ✽
✽

C. Merbvry.

HENRY VNTON,
to the vertuous Reader.

I Ovght not, can not, and therefore will not omit (prouoked by the worthinesse of the matter, compelled by the fast friendship of the Author (whome I haue long, and much loued,) and incouraged by my owne priuate knowledge of the Gentlemans Intent, and trauailes) to publish my priuate good liking, Iudgement, and commendation of this booke: As, a testimoniall of my thankefull good will vnto him: A Seale of our vnfained friendship vnto others: and lastly, a perfecte discharge, and satisfaction for my selfe. Which duely considered I haue burst out into these few rude lines, not to th'Ende I am able to purchasse praise vnto th'Author, (Because the lesse can not authorize the greater) but that I may gaine commendation to my selfe, onely for shew of a thankefull, and well willing minde. Seeing therefore of necessitie I must needes speake somewhat, this is my conceiued opinion: that, in this booke you shall feede your vnderstanding with a most delicate and daintie foode, containing in it a sweete ioyce, and rare Quintessence of the best framed *Monarchie*: wherby the poore of vnderstanding in matters of state may be enriched, and the riche of vnderstanding somewhat therin the better confirmed: and all sortes of men with an admiration of her *Maiesties* most Royall person, and perfect gouernement not a litle rauished: wherunto th'Authors whole intent onely directeth it selfe. And albeit his Discourse be but small in quantitie, yet it exceedeth in qualitie. For that his writing is not obscure, but cleere: not forced, but free: not roughe or harshe, but smoothe, and pleasaunt: not out of order, but well vnited, methodicall, briefe, full fraited with varietie of matter, and nothing at all affected: briefly it is not painted with any glorious colours, but naked, (like the truth,) and in all pointes it is like vnto him selfe: who coueteth rather to be in this his Countrey as a tree in a garden to beare fruite, then as a tree to make a shew and shadow onely. Imploye therefore (I beseeche you) your leasure, to reade with a purged iudgement this his rare Enterprice, and by your good, and iust commendation, rather seeke to spurre others to treade these his good steppes: then by your discommendation to clippe their winges, which else of them selues would make the like flight. Which if you doe, (as if you paye your selues with reason you must needes doe,) you may incourage both him and many others to be your Creditors hereafter for the like, or greater Enterprises.
Fare you well.

A DISCOVRS OF MO-
NARCHIE AS OF THE BEST COM-
mon wealth: tending vnto the duitifull
confideration or rather admiration
of a Royall Princes moſt highe,
and happy Eſtate.

S there is nothing more comfortable vnto all li-uing creatures, then to fee the light, and ſhining of the gladſome Sunne: So is there nothing more ioyful vnto all good ſubiectes, then to beholde the Glorie, and Maieſtie of their foueraigne Prince. If the Sunne intercep-ted with cloudes, and vapours, or by ſome other interpoſition preuēted, ſendeth not forth his lightſome beames: The whole face of the Earth is couered (as we fee it is in the night feaſon) with ſadneſſe, and blacke, and loth-ſome darkneſſe. Birdes keepe in their buſhes, ſnakes in their holes, men hide them ſelues

in their houses. In like maner if the Princes Power be in any pointe impared, or the brightnesse of his Royall Maiestie any whitte eclipsed: the subiecte straight doth feele the smarte, and want therof. The Trauailer is lesse estemed abrode: the Courtier lesse regarded at home: the Marchante lesse priuileged in a farre countrey: the Noble man lesse honored in his owne. For as the Moone, the Starres, and all inferiour lightes doe fetche their light from that great light (the life, and light of the worlde:) Euen so the prosperous estate of the subiectes, is deriued from the prosperitie of the Prince: their honour from his honour: their estimation from his estimation. So long as the Romane Empire flourished, and retained his light, and brightnesse, a Senator of ROME was thought any kinges compagnion : a Citizen, or souldier of ROME might haue trauailed ouer all the worlde without paying one pennie of taxe, or towle. And since the Dignitie of th'Empire was translated into Germany: the Germanes also in most places haue like priuileges. At BOLOGNA (a famous Vniuersitie of the Popes in Lombardie) they are not subiect vnto th'Inquisition: At FLORENCE, SIENNA, PISA, (cheife cities

cities of Tuscane) they haue free libertie to carie their weapons, and in many places they pay no Impostes. So the Spagniard, because his Prince is of great Power, and pretendeth many Titles: he chalengeth also many Preheminences. If he may haue his will, he will sit vppermost at the table wheresoeuer he commeth: and though he haue neither money in his purse, nor good cloathes on his backe: yet because his maister is kinge of Spaine, he wilbe SIGNOR DI CASTILIA: and starue rather, then worke in any maner of way with his hands to get him a liuing. For truely I do not remember that I haue seene any Spagniard, (and yet I haue seene a great many both at MILAN, NAPLES, MESSINA, SYRACVSA, MALTA) euer to exercise out of his countrey any manuall occupation. But I haue founde him, either in the Gallies a souldier, or in the Cities in maner of a Gentleman: wheras th'Italian hauing lost the light, and dignitie of his nation: (the Romane Empire) is contente on the Seas sometimes to play the Mariner, and other whiles in the Cities to sit dressing of silke: So the Fleminge because his countrey seemeth of late yeares to be ouershadowed with a kinde of

A ij

darkeneſſe,(as wanting the foreſaid brightneſſe of Royall Maieſtie) he, as a man halfe in diſgrace, liueth abroade with leſſe reputation: and for the moſt parte vpon ſome bare, and handycrafte occupation.

VVherefore it is no ſmall comforte vnto an Engliſh Gentleman, finding him ſelfe in a farre countrey, when he may boldly ſhew his face, and his forehead vnto any forren Nation : ſit ſide by ſide with the proudeſt Spagniard: cheek by cheeke with the ſtouteſt Germane: ſet foote to foote with the forewardeſt Frenchmā: knowing that his moſt Royall Prince (her Maieſties highneſſe) is no whitte ſubiecte, nor inferiour vnto any of theirs. But that ſhee may alſo (if ſhee plaiſe) chalenge the ſuperioritie both ouer ſome of them, and ouer many other kinges, and Princes more. As maiſter DEE hath very learnedly of late (in certaine tables by him collected out of ſundry auncient, and approued writers) ſhewed vnto her Maieſtie, that ſhee may iuſtly call her ſelfe LADY, and EMPERES of all the Northe Ilandes.

The which kindes of titles, and dignities, although they be not altogether to be neglected, (For they may in conuenient time miniſter iuſt

occa-

occasion vnto the Prince to inlarge his dominions:) yet because they are but as Lanternes without light, or lightes without warmth, as flowers without fruite, and blossomes without substance, or certaintie: they are neither so highly to be regarded, nor so tenderly to be cherished, as those Royalties, and dignities, which I intende (where occasiõ shalbe offered) to commend vnto the excellencie of ROYALL MONARCHIE, as necessarie vnto the framing, and fashioning of a best, and a most perfect common weale: The skope, and marke whervnto tendeth the speciall purpose of this presente discourse. For, as in a morall Treatice I haue done my indeuour to shew what is the principall, and last ende of the best common weale: So doe I desire in this ciuill discourse to declare, what is the best forme, and fashion of the same: And thirdly (when time shall serue) to speake of the discipline, and maner of gouuernement wherwith shee may best direct her selfe vnto the obteining of the saide her last ende and perfection.

Discourses (I confesse) more fit for them that are continually conuersante in the skoole of good learning, or for such, as tredde the pathe of publicke affaires, then for him that followeth no such profession: Yet seeing that I proceede not therin by waye of rules and preceptes: As CICERO, ARISTOTLE, and PLATO did in their common weales, (*Che non vanno si alte l'ale mie,*) but by the way of reasoning, and of discourse, not presuming to teache any (thinking my selfe skante worthy to learne of those vnto whose excellent handes these lines may happely come) but meaning onely to put the learned reader in minde of that, which he already knoweth; and if by chaunce there shall be any thing new therin, and not in this our natiue language before time written, humbly to recommend the same vnto his courteous correction: I hope, my modeste meaning will helpe to excuse the boldnesse of my enterprise, and the courtesie of the reader will vouchsafe to regarde more the good wil, and th'indeuour: then the simple skill, and youngnesse of the writer.

The maner of proceeding of the Author.

But for to come vnto our present Institution: I will first (because there are diuers kindes of common weales, and diuers opinions therof according vnto the diuersitie of mens affections:) before I speake of the maner, and forme of the best common weale: shew in generall, what

The order obserued by the author.

Royall Monarchie.

what a common weale is: how many speciall kindes of common weales there are: and wherin they differre one from an other. A common weale therefore is, An order of gouernement obserued in a citie, or in a countrey, as touching the Magistrates that beare rule therin: especially concerning that Magistrate, which hath highest authoritie, and is the principall. The supreme, or principal Magistrate we meane him, who ruleth all vniuersally: from whome is deriued, & vpon whome dependeth the power, and authoritie of all inferiour offices, and orders: As in a popular Estate, the people: In a kingdome, the Prince. Of commō weales some are good, and iuste, which tende onely vnto th'aduauncement of the publicke profit. Others are ill, and wicked, tending altogether vnto their owne priuate commoditie, and not vnto the benefit of their countrey. Of good common weales there be three kindes. The first is, wheras a number of good men, and men of reasonable wealth, doe iointly beare rule together, procuring by all good meanes they can, the weale of their countrey: the which is called by the generall name of common weale: (in Latine *Respublica*) such as was vsed in SPAR-

What a cōmon weale is.

How many kindes of common weales there are.

What is Respublica.

TA, and is now in GENOA, and in LVCCA.

    An other is, when the gouernemente of the whole is committed vnto the handes of a few of the best, and choisefte persones, such as indeuour to imploye the same vnto the benefitte of those, which are vnder them: The which in the Greeke tongue, is called Αριϛοκρατια: An Eftate of the best, or a gouernement of the states: wherof the common weale of VENICE is at this daye the onely Phenix. The third is that which we call a kingdome, the greekes Μοναρχια: wheras one onely ruleth, and hath soueranitie: directing such his gouernement (next vnto the glorie of God,) vnto the prosperous, and happy estate of his subiectes. Examples wherof, though in these dayes of ours there seeme to be many: (all nations of the worlde almost, hauing receiued this kinde of gouernement) yet we neede not seeke any farther then our owne natiue countrey for a most liuely, and perfecte paterne of the same. And these be the three good common weales, deuised for the maintenaunce of mankinde, established for th'aduancement of iustice; and generally receiued, and imbraced for the prosperitie of cities, and countreys.

What is aristokratia.

What is Monarchie.

                            Now

Now there are as many ill common weales, cleane contrarie vnto these, being in deede nothing else, but the corruptions, and destructiōs, into the which the good common weales doe fall: when they doe alter from the maner, and forme wherin they were first instituted. The first is, when the multitude of the common people, and of the baser sorte, (as of handycraftes men, and such other) haue the maneging of publicke affaires: vsing, or rather abusing such their authoritie vnto th'oppressing of the nobilitie, and aduauncing of the cōmonaltie: fauoring alwayes those, that are of poorest, and meanest condition at their owne foolish fancie, without all order, or discretion. This corrupte, and confuse kinde of gouernemente is called in Greeke δημοκρατία, A state popular: such as was in ROME: when the Tribunes preuailed against the Consulls: and as was in FLORENCE after th'expulsing of PIERRO DE' MEDICI. The second is, where a few of the richest, and of the mightiest, becaufe of their great power, and possessions doe carie all the swaye, seeking onely their owne profit, and not the furtherance of the common weale. The which is called in Greeke Ολιγαρχια: such as was

What is Democratie.

What is Oligarchie

B

in FLORENCE in the yeare 1 4 9 4 : when CHARLES the eighte of France ouerranne Italie subduyng NAPLES: and as was in SIENA in time of the PETRVCCII: and in GENOA in time of the ADORNI, and FREGOSI. The thirde is called TYRANNIE, wheras one onely ruleth at his owne luste, and pleasure, and all for his owne aduauntage: without hauing any regarde vnto the good, or ill estate of his subiectes. As DIONYSIVS did in SIRACVSA: NERO, COMMODVS, CARRACALLA did in ROME: The greate Signori doth in Turkie: and as king VORTIGERNE in the yeare 447. did here in Englande: who for to mainteine his Tyrannie called in the Saxons, and they to stablish their new power: oppressed the Brittons: dryuing them into a corner of the Ilande, brenning, and spoiling their countrey: wheras WILLIAM the Conquerour (a Prince of more Iustice) forbad (at his first arriuall here) his souldiers to hurte, or spoile any Englishman: saying that it should be a great sinne, and follie for him to spoile that people: which ere many dayes after were like to be his subiectes. VVherby we may see, that all good common weales haue alwayes an especiall care, and tendernesse

What is Tyrannie.

dernesse ouer the subiectes, as good fathers haue ouer their children: And the corrupted, and vsurped gouernmentes (like vnto vnnaturall mothers) haue no regarde, but of their owne lustes, and licenciousnesse.

But to speake more particularly of the differences betwene good and ill common weales: VVe finde that a common weale commonly so called, (and taken in good parte) is content with a meane estate, neither enuying others, because she wanteth not her selfe, neither enuyed of any, because she doth not possesse any great aboundance of wealth. (I meane in priuate mens handes:) she is obediente vnto the lawes, not insolent in her magistrates: she is not of so vile, and base minde: as to suffer her selfe to be choked with bribes, or corrupted with couetousnesse. But the Signorie of the mechanicall people, (called DEMOCRATIA) is alwayes in confusion: she enuyeth the riche, and malliceth the mightie, seeking how to betraye the nobilitie: she is of so base, and vile condition: as she can not applie her selfe vnto any kinde of good gouernement: she is ignorant of all thinges: and yet she thinketh to know euery thing: In few wordes she is no bet-

The difference betwene Respublica, & Democratia.

ter then an vniuersall confusion, a horrible monster of many heddes without reason, & a tempestuous Sea tossed with boysterous windes in euery place & at euery season. Betwene the gouernement of the best, and that of the mightiest, there is this difference. Those of the best haue no other ende prefixed vnto them, but vertue and honestie: They refuse no trauaile, or paines for the benefit of such, as are committed vnto their charge: they loue and cherish the poore people, procuring to make them liue in good, and plentifull estate, defending them also from being iniured of mightier, and richer then they: and aboue all thinges they seeke to traine vp their citizens, and subiectes: as they would doe their owne proper children, vnder a continuall discipline of vertue, and good education. These of the mightiest, studie onely how to pull from their subiectes all the wealth vnto them selues: by laying intollerable taxes, and tributes vpon them: All profites, honors, pleasures, and commodities they thinke to be due vnto them onely: All charges, labours, troubles, and dangers postinge ouer vppon the people, whome neuerthelesse they hate deadly: inuenting by all meanes how to intrappe them, and that with all

The difference betwene Aristocratie, and Oligarchie.

kind

Royall Monarchie.

kind of insolencie. Betwene a good Kinge, and a Tyrante there is this difference. The one is courteous, mercifull, endewed with all vertue: the other is hautie, and cruell, defiled with all vice. The one embraceth equitie, and iustice: the other treadeth both Gods lawe, and mans lawe vnder his feete. The one hath his minde, and all his care vpon the health, and wealth of his subiectes: th'other estemeth his owne pleasure more then their profit, his owne wealth, more then their good willes. The good Kinge taketh pleasure to be freely aduertised, and wisely reprehended when he doth amisse: the Tyrante can abide nothing worse, then a graue, free spoken, and a vertuous man. The good Kinge punisheth publicke iniuries, and pardoneth those which are done vnto him selfe: the Tyrante reuengeth most cruelly his owne iniuries, neglecting those, which are done vnto others. The good King hath an especiall regarde vnto the honour, and good name of chaste matrones: the Tyrant triumpheth in abusing, and shaming of them. The good Kinge deliteth to be seene, and otherwhiles hard of his subiectes: the Tyrant hideth him selfe from them, as from his enemies. The good Kinge loueth his people

The difference betwene Monarchie, & Tyrannie.

B iij

and is beloued of them againe: the Tyrant neither loueth them, that are like vnto himselfe fearing left they being as wicked as he, will be ready to betray him for euery light cause, & he hateth, and pursueth all those that haue any valor, or vertue in them: as men, whome he knoweth to be by nature contrarie, and enemies vnto his tyrannie. Againe the one chargeth his people as litle as he can, and but vpon publicke honorable and necessarie occasions: the other gnaweth the bones, and sucketh out the very blood, and marowe of them with vnlawfull taxes, towles, and confiscations: The one maketh choise of the best, and most sufficient persones about him to imploye in the publicke affaires: the other imployeth none but ruffianes, and cutthrotes: such as he may best serue his owne turne withall: The one vseth the assured fayth and forces of his owne subiectes, in time of warre against his enemies: the other calleth in forreine nations whome he can not safely trust: (as LODOVIKO SFORZA duke of MILANE did) to warre against his owne contreymen: The one hath no garde, nor garrison but of his owne naturall people: the other but of strangers: The one liueth in assured hope, merrie, voide

Royall Monarchie.

voide of suspition, alwayes enioying the sweete rewarde of his vpright conscience: the other hath the pointe of a sworde hanging ouer his head: alwayes languishing in continuall feare: The one looketh for euerlasting ioye: the other can hardly escape euerlasting paine: The one is honored in his life time, and wished for after his death: the other is hated in his life time, and torne in peeces, after he is deade: so that liuing, and dying he is in a continuall hell of all miserie. Wherefore as the gouernement of a Tyrant is of all other the most odious, and of the three ill common weales the worst: So is a Lawefull kingdome of the three good the best, the happiest, and that which I desire to preferre in this my Treatice before all other: Not ledde therunto onely by bonde of duetie, as subiecte, and seruant vnto so worthy a Prince: Nor moued by affection onely, as borne in so quiet, and prosperous estate of countrey: But moued, ledde, and drawen by force of good reason, grounded vpon the naturall excellencie, and excellent propertics therof: as it shall at large appeare: after that I haue first shewed of what especiall kinde and qualitie this best common weale of kindome is.

Which is the best common weale.

Sundry kindes of Monarchies.

For there are diuers kindes of kingdomes, according vnto the diuersitie of countryes, and of their lawes, and customes: though all good, & lawfull, yet not all of like excellencie: though all pertakers of soueranitie, yet not all in equall proportion: though of like nature, and essence, yet differing accidētally. *Kingdomes by Gifte.* For some kingdomes go by gifte, as IVBA was by OCTAVIVS, made of a slaue kinge of NVMIDIA (now called Barbarie:) and as the kingdomes of NAPLES, and SICILE were giuen first vnto CHARLES Earle of Prouence in the yeare 1266. and after vnto LEWIS the first Duke of Anioue brother vnto the french kinge CHARLES the fifth, (surnamed the wise:) and as some haue written that WILLIAM the Conquerour by the gifte of his Nephew kinge EDWARD sonne of king EGELRED pretended, and attained vnto the Crowne of England. *Kingdomes by Testamente.* Others are lefte by will of testament, as CHARLES Nephew, and heire vnto RENALD Duke of Anioue bequethed all his estates, and dominions vnto the french *Kingdomes by Customes.* kinge LEWIS the leuenth. Some descende by the vertue of a Lawe, as the Realme of Fraunce in practise of late descentes doth by the Lawe which they call SALICKE. Others goe by adoption,

Royall Monarchie.   17

doption, as EGEVS kinge of ATHENES adop- *Kingdomes*
ted THESEVS: MICIPSA kinge of the Nu- *by Adoptiō.*
midians adopted IVGVRTHA: SCIPIO th'el-
der adopted the sonne of PAVLVS ÆMILIVS:
CÆSAR the dictator, his Nephew: AVGV-
STVS th'Emperor, adopted TIBERIVS: CLAV-
DIVS, NERO: NERVA, TRAIAN: TRAIAN,
ADRIAN, who after adopted ANTONINVS
(surnamed the Pityfull:) & so were ÆLIVS VE-
RVS, and MARCVS AVRELIVS also adopted
vnto th'Empire. Likewise of late yeares ANNE,
and IANE Queenes of NAPLES, and SICIL-
LE adopted LEWIS, aud RENALTE Duke of
Anioue: and in the yeare 1408. MARGARIT
Queene of Demnarke, and Swethlande adopted HENRY Duke of Pomerane for their
heires, and successours in all their dominitions.
So in king HENRY the fifth of England byside
the interest of his auncesters, and his owne interest vnto the Crowne of France was added an
adoption by his father in law the french kinge
CHARLES the sixte. Some kingdomes are *Kingdomes*
translated from one to an other by lotte, or *by Lotte.*
chaunce of fortune: as it happened vnto DA-
RIVS one of the seuen Lordes of PERSIA, who
was made kinge, because his horse first neyed.

C

Kingdomes by Pollicie. Some estates are gotten by Pollicie, as in olde time CECROPES, HIERON, GELON, PISISTRATVS gotte theirs: and as of later yeares COSMVS of MEDICES added the state of SIENNA vnto his Dukedome of FLORENCE.

Kingdomes by Cōquest. A number of kingdomes also are gotten by conqueste: As FERDINAND of ARAGON the first king of Spaine got the kingdomes of NAPLES, NAVARRA, SICILE: and after him his daughters sonne CHARLES the fifte, got the kingdome of THVNES, the dukedome of MILAN, the Soueranitie of Artois, and Flanders.

Kingdomes by Election. Others go by Election, as the kingdome of POLONIA doth. And of this kinde there are diuers sortes: For some are chosen kinges for their Noblenesse of birthe: As CAMPSON kinge of Caramania, was by the Mammelucs chosen for their SOVLDANE: the Vycountes of ANGLERIE were for their noble birth made Lordes of MILANE: Some for their Iustice, as NVMA POMPILIVS was by the Romaines: Some for their olde age, as the auncient ARABIANS did choose alwayes the eldest: Some for their great possessions, and mightie power: As HARAVLDE (sonne to GOODWINNE Earle of Kente) was after the death of kinge

E-

EDWARD (surnamed the Sainte becauſe of the good, and wholeſome lawes, which he in this our countrey inſtituted) choſen the laſt SAXON kinge in Englande : Some for their ſtrenght of body: as MAXIMINVS: Others for their beautie, as HELIOGABALVS: Others for their greatneſſe, and tallneſſe of ſtature, As they were wonte to doe in ÆTHIOPIA. All which are kindes of kingdomes, and they may be good, and lawfull, according as they are well and lawfully vſed: But they are not of that excellencie which is required in our beſt kingdome. For there is yet an other kinde farre more excellent, then any of them, more commendable, more ſure, leſſe ſubiect to corruptiō, more capable of perfection. VVhich is when a kingdome deſcendeth by right of Succeſſion vnto the next of the blood royall. In the which point we are cōtent to ſwarue from him, whom hitherto in the waye of Philoſophie we haue moſt followed: who was of opinion that kinges were rather to be choſen, calling them people Barbarous, which did take their kinges by way of Succeſſion : preferring therefore the Carthaginians before the Lacedemonians, becauſe theſe receiued their kinges by Succeſſion, thoſe

Which is the beſt kinde of Kingdome

That Succeſſion is to be preferred before Election.

by Election. But perhappes ARISTOTLE would haue differed herein from him selfe: if he had liued a litle longer for to haue sene how the MONARCHIE of Macedone (hauing continued fiue hundreth yeares from the father vnto the sonne in the right Line of HERCVLES) was after for want of Royall and Lineall Succession brought vnto vtter confusion. Or if he had liued in these dayes of ours, to haue seene how kingdomes goe now, how they florish, how amplie they distēde them selues, he would (doubtlesse) haue changed his opinion, and neuer haue called Barbarous so many goodly countryes, and so diuers sondry sortes of nations: both of ASIA (as the Persians, Medians, Parthenians, Turkes, Tartarres, Arabians:) of AFRICA (the Æthiopians, Barbarians, Numidians:) of EVROPE, (England, Scotland, Fraunce, Spaine, Naples, Sicile,) preferring before all th'afore saide riche and florishing Estates a few colde countryes of Polonia, Demnarke, and Swethland: because these haue their kinges by Election, those by Succession. But he neuer needed for to haue liued so long for this matter. For if he would but haue looked backe with an indifferent eye into his owne coun-

countrey of Greece (the which he commended to be so ciuill) he should haue found, that th'Athenians, Lacedemonians, Sicyonians, Corinthians, Thebanes, Epirotes, Macedonians, for the space of sixe hundreth yeares neuer had any other gouernement, but of kinges, and those by the right, and lawfull waye of Succession: vntill such time, as ambition, pride, and priuate Interest blinded their vnderstanding, and made them change their kingdomes into DEMOCRATIES, and ARISTOCRATIES misterming the same by the false name of libertie. The like may be said of the auncient Toscanes, and of the olde Latines, who many hundreth yeares before the building of ROME had their kinges, and gouernours descending lineally one vnto an other. As we reade that ÆNEAS by the right of his wife succeded vnto LATINVS: TIBERIVS (of whome the riuer of Teuer or Tyber which runneth by ROME was so named) vnto ÆNEAS: and so forth vntill the kingdome came to ROMVLVS by the waye of his mother RHEA (daughter to NVMITOR. and Nece to AMVLIVS kinges of the Latines.) VVhereby we maye gather that in those dayes neither Election was vsed, nor yet any exception made of kinde or Gender. But some man will say. O how happy is that coūtrey, where the estates of the people do make choise of a iust, and righteous Prince, who feareth God aboue all thinges, honoreth vertue, oppresseth vice, giueth rewarde vnto the good, and punishment vnto the wicked, that hateth flatterers, keepeth his fayth, and his promisse, banisheth out of his Courte the Inuentours of new exactions, reuengeth the iniuries that are done vnto others, & forgiueth those that are done vnto him selfe. These are faire speeches, and they seeme to cary with them great good apparences. *Sed latet anguis in herba*, they shew not *id manticæ quod in tergo est*. But as we are wonte to carie alwayes two sachelles about vs, one before, to put other mens faultes in, and an other behinde, wherin to hide our owne: So they make no mention of the daungers, and discommodities which are incident vnto such kinde of Elections. As what

What Incōueniences do proceede from Elections. a monsterous Inconuenience is that when *Sede vacante*, after the Prince is deade, and before a new can be chosen, the whole state remaineth in a very ANARCHIE, without kinge, or any kinde of gouernement, like a shippe without a Pilote in hazarde to be cast awaye with euery winde:

winde: Then may you see all lewdnesse, and licentiousnesse set at libertie: Theeues robbe by the highe way side without punishment, Murderers commit their treasons without controllment. For the first thing that is done *Sede vacante* is to breake open the prisons, kill the iaylors, reuenge iniuries, oppresse the poore with all insolent, and vniust meanes. As we reade that the MAMMELVCS were wont to doe sacking, and spoiling the poore people of EGYPTE whilest their SOVLDANE was a choosing. And this Impunitie of vice for the most parte lasteth vntill such time, as the ELECTORS doe fall to agreement: which happeneth not some times in a yeare or twaine, otherwhiles not in tenne. The Empire of Germanie laie voide 18. yeares together after the death of th'Emperor VVILLIAM Earle of Holande: The Sea of ROME after the death of CLEMENT the fifte remained two yeares, and a halfe without any Pope: after NICHOLAS the third three yeares: after Pope IOHN fiue yeares: and sometimes the Sea hath bene vacant tenne yeares together. In all the which time a Romane coulde not stirre out of his dores without daunger: a stranger could not trauaile on the highe wayes without perill of his life. And at this daye there are so many FVORVSCITI vpon the borders, as that no man will ryde betwene ROME, and NAPLES without the PROCACCIO, and 40. or 50. horse in his companie: VVheras in euery other parte of ITALIE that I haue bene in (and I haue bene in the most parte,) a man may ryde safly with his purse in the palme of his hande. But you will saye, that there may be therefore in time of vacation, A gouernour apointed to administer Iustice, and to punish vice: So shall all this tempestuous Sea be quieted, & all those mischiefes remedied. I graunt well: but yet with a greater mischiefe. For if the gouernement be committed vnto one only with absolute power, and authoritie to rule, and commaunde vntill the Prince be elected: let me aske you, who shall lette such a one, as hath the lawe in his owne handes to make him selfe if he liste of a gouernour a king: as GOSTAVVS father vnto IOHN kinge of Swethlande did. If he haue Legions of souldiers at his commaundement, who shall let him from making him selfe of a Consull for a time, a Dictator for euer: as IVLIVS CÆSAR did. Againe if the gouernement be laide during th'Election vpon sundry persones, as it is now

How daungerous a gouernour is, Sede vacante.

now vſed in POLONIA, and as it was wonte to be ſome times in ROME: The daunger is no leſſe, leſt the mightieſt of them, that haue ſuch power laie not handes vpon the Fortreſſes, and ſtrongeſt holdes of the Countrey: As POMPEIO COLONNA, and ANTONIO SAVELLA did, who in the like caſe ſeazed vpon the CAMPIDOLLE, crying vnto the people of ROME, Libertie, Libertie. So we ſee that the woundes are well nighe incurable, which ſuch countries receiue at the death of their Princes: The paines are no leſſe, and the daungers as great, or greater, which they ſuſtaine in chooſing of their new kinges. As what a worlde of trouble was that of late yeares in the kingdome of POLONIA about th'Election, when the Pollackes were faine to ſende into Fraunce (ſo many miles, thorough ſo many countryes) for the Duke of Anioue (now HENRY the third of Fraunce) to be their king: and what ſucceſſe all their paines, and trauailes had who knoweth it not? Did not the Duke ſo ſoone, as his brother CHARLES dyed, & that a greater kingdome fell vnto him, leaue them, and retourne into his owne countrey: (as right and reaſon would, that a man ſhould be more carefull of his owne Nation, *Troubles and daungers incidente vnto Elections.*

then of ſtrangers.) And the like did LODOVIKE kinge of Hungarie before him, who being choſen, and crowned kinge of Polonia, retourned ſtraight after into his owne countrey: leauing a Lieftenante behinde him to gouerne the Polonians withall. A thing odious vnto men of valour, and greuous vnto all free people: when they can not ſee the face, and countenance of their Soueraine Prince: but muſt be controlled with the pride, and ouerlayed with the couetuouſneſſe of inferiour Magiſtrates. The which burden how vnwillingly it is borne MILAN, NAPLES, SIENA, SICILE, and FLANDERS to their coſt, and paine haue knowen.

But let vs imagine that a Prince, hauing two kingdomes, one by ſucceſſion, an other by Election, and being lothe to leaue either of them, will make what ſhifte he can to be perſonally reſidente vpon them both: (the which he can hardly doe, excepte they be very neere adioyning one to the other:) who doubteth then, but that he will make (if he can) one kingdome of them both, or of both kingdomes one MONARCHIE. As CHARLES the fifth, would haue done with the countryes of Germanie, hauing brought his ſonne PHILIPPE, purpoſely into thoſe

those partes, for to haue made him king of the Germanes, if the french kinge HENRY the first had not by aiding of them, distourned him from that his pretended and commenced course. But though th'Emperour was of that his purpose so disapointed, and could not be suffred to vnite the countryes of Germany vnto his other kingdomes: yet it is well knowen, that he lost not all the benefitte of his Election, nor all his labour, and time in vaine, which he bestowed in those partes. But so long as he liued, and sate in the seat of th'Empire, their are many that can yet remember, how he made his Haruest of them, and rept what commodities he could of the said countryes, drawing forth of them from time to time, both men, money, and Munition to serue his other priuate purposes withall. As in his Italian warres against the French king FRANCES the first he had at one time vnder the conducte of CHARLES of BORBONE his Lieftenant 18. thousand at the left of the Dutch Nation: By meanes of whome, and of a few Spagniardes more, he droue the French men out of all their possessions in Lombardie, he impatroned him selfe of the Dukedome of MILANE: he impropriated to his one vses the Ci-

D ij

ties of PARMA, and PIACENZA: he altered for his owne aduantage the states of FLORENCE, SIENA, and of GENOVA: he sacked ROME: and in briefe, by meanes of the Germaines he subdued and brought all Italie vnder his yoke. In like maner when he went to ALGIERS (An enterprise which could no kinde of waye benefit the Germaine Nation, no nor yet any whit the Estate of Christendome, but tending altogether vnto the benefit, and aduancement of his owne countryes of Spaine) he vsed not onely the bodies, but the goods, and substance also of the Germaines: causing them by waye of a Counsell or Diette (which he called purposely to the same end) to contribute vnto the charges of that his glorious voiage. He was therefore a Prince, if you regarde the greatnesse of his minde, the hautinesse of his Enterprises, the number of his victories, the hugenesse of his possessions, his valour, his wisedome, and his temperance, he was (I say) a Prince most worthie, of that fame, and great name, which he caried in the mouth, and th'opiniō of the world. But if you looke into his doinges, and whereto they tended, you shall finde, (and I haue heard an honorable personage that knew him well,

Glorious in the setting forth thereof, though not in the sequelle, & successe of the same.

Royall Monarchie.

well, and most of his proceedinges, affirme the same) that he was the lest beneficiall Emperour vnto the common weale of Christendome, and the most hard, and heauy Prince vnto the states of Germanie, of a great many others, that went before him, and of any that as yet are come after him. For it appeareth that he directed all his actions vnto the stablishing, and stengthning of those Estates onely, which he knew should necessarily descend vnto his lawfull and lyneall heyres after him, litle or nothing regarding the succession of them, which were to be elected at the will and pleasure of others. VVherefore as he fetched both men, and money out of Germanie, for to serue his other tournes withall abroade: so tooke he from thence also (A thing which I my selfe haue hard much lamented by the Germaines) the best parte of all their Munition: As out of VVITTEMBOVRGE (a citie of the Duke of SAXON) he tooke two hundreth and twentie peeces of great Ordinance: a hundreth out of GOTTA: from the LANGRAVE also he had 200. peeces: and out of STRAVSBOVRGH, he tooke all the best, that they had: Sending thereof 50. peeces vnto NAPLES, other 50. to MILANE, and 400.into

FLANDRES: he did the like also with many other their Dutche Commodities, transporting them, either into SPAINE, or into his countries of AVSTRICH, for to inlarge, and make riche his owne house and posteritie withall. And this is a thing common vnto all elected Princes (that haue Estate but for terme of Life) carelesly to cōsume the Treasores of the countrey, dissipating the publicke demaines, and conuerting them into priuate mens handes, either of their owne fauorites, or of their kinsefolkes. As of the Cities, and Prouinces belonging vnto the Sea of ROME, the Popes haue made awaye almost the one halfe for the aduauncement of their owne priuate houses. Pope SIXTVS the fourth of that Name, after the death of GVIDIBALDO DE MONTEFELTRO Duke of VRBYNE, procured the dukedome vnto his kinseman de ROVERE. The which dukedome (not long after) Pope LEO the tenth, translated from FRANCESCO MARIA DE ROVERE vnto his Nephew LORENZO DE' MEDICI. Pope ALEXANDER the sixte gaue REGIO, and MODENA (two good Townes in Italie) in dowrie with his daughter vnto ALFONSO Duke of FERRARA. CLE-

How countryes are impouerished by Princes elected.

MENT

Royall Monarchie.

MENT the seuenth, aduanced his Nephew ALEXANDRO vnto the Dukedome of Florence. And PAVLVS tertius the Romane exalted his house of FARNESE vnto the Dukedome of PARMA, and PIACENZA: All which Estates were either conueyed out of the Ecclesiasticall Monarchie, or by the meanes, and charge therof procured. As GVICCIARDINE in his storie of the warres of ITALIE reporteth that the forenamed LEO the tenth, what with warring against the duke of VRBYNE, and with mainteining the costlinesse of his sister MAGDALENA, and his owne pride, and prodigalitie, he left the Church worse by 40. thousand Ducates a yeare, then he found it: besides the iewells, and ornamentes of the pontificall treasor, which he engaged. In the like maner all Temporall Princes (I meane such as are elected) when they see that they can not leaue their estates vnto their Children, they seeke by sale, or by gifte to make the best commoditie of them during their owne liues. As RODVLPHVS th'Emperour for a summe of money exempted all the Cities of TOSCANE out of the subiection of th'Empire. And ROBERT OF BAVIER gaue three Imperiall cities at one time vnto his sonne

FREDERIKE, he gaue alſo the Liberties vnto NVRENBOVRGE. As OTHO the third did vnto ISNE. LODOWIKE of BAVIER did the like vnto the citie of EGRE. HENRY the firſt ſoulde what he coulde, whereby th'Empire was brought ſo low, as that CHARLES duke of Burgony was able to make warre againſt the whole bodie of the ſame. If then an Italian will not ſticke to weaken the Popedome, (the pride and ſtrength of his Nation:) nor a Germaine to deminiſh the power of th'Empire, (a Dignitie which the Germanes pretende to be dewe, and proper vnto them onely:) Much leſſe may we thinke that a Hungarian will obſerue any more reſpecte in Polonia, being choſen vnto that kingdome: or a Spagniarde vſe any more courteſy in Italy, being elected vnto the Popedome: But rather it is to be thought that they, ſeeing them ſelues called by this vnorderly way of Election vnto new gouernementes, will ſeeke for the better ſtabliſhing of the ſame, to alter in what they can the ſtate, and courſe of the countryes, wheruynto they are ſo called: tourning their lawes, into theirs: their cuſtomes, into theirs: their Religion, into their owne Religion. For commonly we ſee that all men are of that

nature

nature to thinke alwayes their owne religion best, their owne customes commēdablest, their owne lawes soundest: desiring to bring and induce al others vnto the same lawes, customes, & religiō that they them selues are of. The Turke would haue all his people to acknowledge Mahomet: The kinge of Spaine all his subiectes to holde with the Pope: The Greekes thought all other nations barbarous in respecte of them selues. The Italians likewise in these dayes are not ashamed to call all *Oltramontani* (vs that are on this side the Alpes) *barbari*, as though none knew what Ciuilitie mente but they. The Venetians will say, when they heare a man speake in a language which they vnderstand not, *Mo! parlate Christiano*, as though no language were good or christianlike but theirs. So, William the Conquerour sought to surpresse, and extinguish our English speeche, commaunding all our lawes to be writtē in his owne language, as it appeareth also by the termes of our pastimes (of hawking, hunting, karding, dycing, Tennis, and such like,) which for the most parte doe yet remaine in the Normane tongue. VVherfore it is euident that all elected Princes, which come out of forreine Countryes (in the

E

maner as we here meane (to the ende to rule, and raigne onely, and not for loue, alliance, or freindſhip ſake) will in what lyeth in them, both for their greater glorie, & for the better ſtrength of their Eſtates, ſeeke to change the Religion, lawes, cuſtomes, and language of the places whervnto they are ſo elected. But you will ſay, that your meaning is not to fetch your Prince ſo farre of, but to haue him neerer home euen of the ſame countrey, wherof he is to reigne: becauſe you will be ſure that he ſhall neither change cuſtomes, not bring in any language. You ſay well, but let me aſke then: who ſhall haue the chooſing of him there at home in his owne countrey? If the common people chooſe him, you may looke for nothing elſe, but factions, ſeditions (*Tot capita, tot ſententiæ*) ſo many men, ſo many kinges. If he be choſen by the Souldiers, as the Emperours were otherwhiles of ROME, then ſhall he not be allowed of by the Senatours: if elected by the Senatours: then can he not be receiued of the Souldiers. VVhich inconueniences being of later yeares better wayed of by the wiſer, It was thought expedient, that the Election of th'Empire ſhould be reduced vnto a certaine number

ber of seuen Princes (who, because the Pope as then GREGORIE the fifth, was a SAXON borne were all appointed of the Germaine nation: Namely the duke of SAXON, the Counte PALLATINE, the Marchese of BRANDINBOVRGE, the three Bishoppes of MAGANZA, COLLENE, and TREVERIE, and the seuenth (to waye downe the ballances) the kinge of BOEMIA.) And yet for all that the Electours were neuer so few: the factions, and ciuill discordes that ensued were neuer a whit the lesse. LEWIS of BAVIER, and ALBERTE of AVSTRIKE were both chosen Emperours at one time: whervpon they continued 18. yeares in warres one against the other. In like maner the Colledge of the Cardinalles haue bene (as is before saide) sometimes two, sometimes three yeares together in choosing of one Pope: And at an other time they haue chosen three at a clappe, and oftentimes two together. VVherfore they are now faine to shutte them selues into the CONCLAVE of Saint Peters Pallaice: there to remaine vntill the two thirdes of them do fall to agreement. As it is also more straightly obserued at MALTA (now called VALETTA) in the choosing of the great Maister of the

Difficulties and dissentions, in the choosing of Princes.

E ij

order of Saint IOHN. For there the 24. Electours (appointed by the KNIGHTES of the great Croſſe) are walled into a ſtrong place, where within a certaine time limited vnto them they muſt without all delaye, chooſe one that is not of their number. So we ſee, that the difficulties, and diſſentions which proceede from ſuch Elections are infinite: The Murders alſo and maſſacres that do inſue of them are no leſſe frequent both amongeſt th'Eccleſiaſticall Prelates, and temporall Princes. Of Popes there haue bene at the leaſt 22. beheaded about their Election (as the Regiſters of the VATTICANE doe certifie) beſides a number of Cardinalles, and of common people that for the like cauſe haue gon the ſame waye with them. VVe reade that in the Primatiue Church there were 600. Romanes ſlaine at one time about the chooſing of DAMASVS, and VRSINVS. Of temporall Princes there haue bene within theſe 360. yeares (ſince th'Empire fell into the ſubiection of the Lordes Electours) eight, or nine EMPEROVRS ſlaine and poiſoned. Of 15. SOVLDANES that haue bene choſen kinges of EGYPTE ſeuen of them dyed with the ſworde. Of Romane Emperours after the death of Av-

A number of Popes, & Emperours murdered about their Election.

GVSTVS

GVSTVS there were seuen all in a rowe murdered, and three of them in one yeare. It would greeue me to rehearse, and weary you to heare all the piteous examples, which might be recited in this behalfe: wherof both English, Latine, and Italian histories are euery where full. These few may suffice to shew what slaughters, Murders, Massacres haue bene cōmitted about the choosing of Princes. Neither could there any order be found, either for the sauftie of a kinge, or for the quietnesse of a kingdome, vntill such time, as a lawfull sonne, or sonne made by Adoption, succeded vnto his father without any further Election. As TIBERIVS, TITVS, TRAIAN, ADRIAN, ANTONINVS PIVS, MARCVS AVRELIVS, who all succeded prosperously one vnto th'other in the Romane Empire. The Germaines also (for all their great Titles of Election) are faine at the last to flye vnto this refuge and to fetche their sauftie, and quietnesse from Succession: Suffering the house of AVSTRIKE these hundreth, and three skore yeares solely, and succesfiuely to possesse th'Empire. As after SIGISMONDE, FREDERIKE, then MAXIMILIAN, then CHARLES the fifth, then FERDINANDE, then MAXIMILIAN the

The benefit of Succession.

Kingdomes assured by meanes of Succession.

E iij

seconde, and so vnto RADVLPHE who now raigneth. In POLONIA likewise, BOHEMIA, HONGARIE & DENMARKE, where the states stand so much vpon their Priuileges, they are glad, and faine (of later yeares) for the auoiding of ciuill warres, and other of the aforesaid inconueniences to acknowledge the benefit of this Succession: choosing for the most part him that is next of the blood Royall, and next of kinne vnto the predecessed kinge. So precious a thing it is, as they that hate it, are constrayned to seeke it: And they that haue it, are glad to holde it. SPAINE, NAPLES, CICILLE, NAVARRA, SCOTLAND, and FRAVNCE also (whose Lawe SALIKE for ought, that I can see is nothing else but a limited, or nice kinde of Succession) haue not for these many yeares knowen any other kinde of gouernement. But of all nations there is none that more amplie hath enioyed it, and which doth more willingly reteine it then our owne. Seeing therefore that Lineall Succession is so sure a foundation, as all good kingdomes both do, and may boldly builde theron: And contrarily ELECTION so weake a sande or rather so daungerous a Sea, as it is able to sinke the tallest shippe of Citie,

How Succession is tendered in England.

or

Royall Monarchie. 39

or Countrey that faileth therin: it is good reason that in this our difcourfe of ROYALL MONARCHIE (as we defire to frame the fame the beft, and the moft perfecte common weale) we embrace the one, as a fure grounde, and fhunne the other as a moft daungerous fande, preferring Succeffion before Election, and confequētly before all the other forenamed kindes of kingdomes: the which all are either kindes of Election, or elfe they are of leffe importance, and fuch as are not to be eftemed for their owne worthyneffe, but for fome Neceffitie fake. As where Succeffion faileth, that there is none lefte of the bloode Royall mall, nor femall to inheritte the Crowne, then men are faine to goe to drawing of Lottes, to Neyinge of horfes, to choofing the Nobleft, the wifeft, the Eldeft, the Mightieft, the Richeft. But the beft, and moft Royall Prince is not to receiue his Scepter by any fuch happe, or hazarde of fortune (as DARIVS did his:) Nor to come to his kingdome by the vncertaintie of voices (as all chofen Princes doe:) Nor yet by Gifte, by Cuftome, by Pollicie, or by Conqueft (as it hath bene faide that kinge IVBA, Duke COSIMVS, and many other Princes did come to theirs:) But he is to come vnto his Crowne, and kingdome first, and principally by the grace of GOD, and secondarily by the waye of lawfull, and Lineall SVCCESSION.

It followeth that we speake of the maner of estate of this most ROYALL MONARCHIE: and best kinde of kingdome: (*Come sta* how, and in what case it standeth, as touching the Power, and authoritie appertaining thervnto.) For it is not sufficient that so ROYALL a Prince be descended Lineally, and lawfully into his kingdome: But he must also possesse, and exercise such ROYALL, and princely Power therin, as is most fitte for his worthynesse, and for his subiectes happynesse: Neither in so extreame maner, as to make A god of him selfe (as ALEXANDER the great would haue done,) and slaues of his vassalles (as the Great TVRKE at this daye doth:) Neither yet in so slender sorte, as to haue the sworde caried after him (as the Duke of VENICE hath,) and to be but a litle better, then a sipher, or shadowe of a Prince.

What power appertaineth vnto a Royall Prince.

He is for to haue therefore (by the grace, and Permission of Almightie God) that Power, which the Greekes call Ακραν ἐξουσιαν: the Latines MAIESTATEM: Th'Italians SIGNORIA: The French-

Royall Monarchie.

Frenchmen SOVVERAINETE: That is, Powerfull and perpetuall ouer all his subiectes in generall, and ouer euery one in particular. Not to rule for a yeare onely, as the Consulles of ROME did: Nor for two yeares, as the Dukes of GENOVA doe: Nor for three, as the VICEROYES of NAPLES: or for nine, or ten yeares, as the great Archon of ATHENES did: Not to be DICTATOVR for a daye onely, as MAMERCVS was: Nor for eight dayes, as SERVILIVS PRISCVS: or for fifteen, as CINCINNATVS: No nor yet for fifteen yeares, as SILLA had gotten it graunted vnto him by a Lawe to be Dictatour fourescore yeares (although he raigned but foure:) and then after the terme of yeares expired, to render vp his gouernement vnto an other, perhappes vnto a stranger, perhappes vnto his enemie: But his Power shall last (by Gods grace) perpetually: first during his owne life in him selfe, and then after his death in his sonnes, and successors. *A Royall Prince is to rule without limitatiō of time.*

Neither is he countable of such his gouernement, (sauing to God, and his Conscience) elfe not vnto any other: in such sorte, As LEGATES, LIEFTENANTES, PRESIDENTES, & REGENTS are, who though they haue autho- *A Royall Prince is not Countable vnto Any.*

F

ritie sometimes during their liues, yet are they to render accoumpte vnto those which gaue them the same. The DOGES of VENICE, if they gouerne not well, are deposed by the SIGNORIE of the gentlemen: as TEODATVS, and GALLA of MALOMOCCO were banished, and had their eyes putte out, because they ruled to Lordly. The Gouerners of BOLOGNA LA GRASSA, when they goe out of their office, are bounde to render accoumpte vnto two SYNDICI: The Dictators of ROME were forced by the TRYBVNES to render reason vnto the People. The Regentes of SCOTLANDE, the Lordes Protectors of ENGLAND, although they rule neuer so highly during the minoritie of their Princes: Yet we see that after they are out of their Offices, they are constrained to aunswere vnto many oppositions. There was neuer greater, and more absolute Power graunted vnto any subiecte, then was by CHARLES the ninth, vnto his brother HENRY Duke of ANIOVE, when he made him his Lieftenant Generall, and perpetuall ouer all his dominions: And yet was there in th'ende of his letters patentes this Clause apposed *Tant qu'il nous plaira*, to signifie that the Dukes authoritie was

both

both countable, and reuocable at the will and pleasure of the kinge the giuer. Our Prince therefore is not to receiue his power from any (excepte from God the giuer of all Power:) For if he receiue it from any other higher Prince, then is he not the Principall, and supreame Magistrate, but there is an other higher, and greater then he. For as honour dependeth more of the giuer, then of the receiuer: So likewise that Power is greatest, from whence the others are deriued. But our Prince, who is the Image of God on Earth, and as it were *Vn minor essempio* of his almightie Power, is not to acknowledge any greater then him selfe: nor any authoritie greater then his owne. VVherefore as he is not to receiue his Power from any: so is he neither to be subiect vnto any higher Power, either at home, or abroade: Though some doe mainteine that a Prince ought to be subiect vnto the states and Peares of his Realme: as the kinges of LACEDEMON were to the EPHORI, An Opinion (if it be not well tempered, and conueniently limited) most preiudiciall vnto th'estate of a MONARCHIE: peruerting, and conuerting the same into a meere ARISTOCRATIE: Much lesse is he subiecte in any thing

A Royall Prince is not to depende vpon any.

A Royall Prince is not subiecte vnto any of his owne Countrey.

vnto the Multitude of the common people: who as they haue more authoritie are for the most parte more infolente, and more difpofed vnto rebellion. VVherefore in all wel ordained kingdomes thefe haue no other then a voice SVPPLICATIVE, thofe a voice DELIBERATIVE, and the Prince onely a voice DEFINITIVE.

But fome will afke, if this great MONARCHE of ours fhall not be fubiecte vnto the Lawes, Cuftomes, and Priuileges of the Countrey where he gouerneth: vnto the othe which he taketh at his entrance: vnto fuch couenantes, and promifes as he maketh vnto his people. Vnto whome we aunfwere that our Prince is fubiect vnto lawes both ciuill, and common, to cuftomes, priuileges, couenantes, and all kinde of promifes, So farre forth as they are agreable vnto the lawe of God: Otherwife we thinke that he is not bounde to obferue them. VVherein we neither diminifhe the libertie of the fubiecte, fuppofing all lawes to be good, or ought to be good: Neither doe we inlarge to much the Power of the Prince, as to make him lawleffe, fubiect neither to God his lawe, nor mans lawe. As fome flaterers perfuade the

How a Prince is fubiect vnto the Lawes.

Po-

POPES, and EMPEROVRS that they are aboue all lawes, and may vfe the bodyes, and liues of their fubiectes at their lufte and pleafure, taking from them their landes, goodes, and liberties without right, or reafon: a thing expreffely contrarie vnto the worde of God (Thou fhalt not couet thy neighbours houfe &c.) and a doctrine moft pernicious vnto Princes, who puffed vp with fuch opinions fhould take their courfe vnto a Tyrannicall kinde of puiffance, making their couetoufneffe confifcation, their loue Adulterie, their hatred Murder: and as the lightening goeth before the thunder, fo they depraued with fuch corrupted Councellers fhould make the accufation to goe before the faulte, and the condemnation before the tryall. From the which kindes of libertie, or rather licentioufneffe our ROYALL Prince fhalbe as farre of, as he is free from all kinde of fubiection both domefticall, and forreine. For it is not enough for fo worthy a kinge to be obeyed of his owne people at home, but he muft be alfo well eftemed of ftrangers abroade: not onely beloued of his freindes, but honoured of his neighbours, and feared of his enemies. VVherfore, as we haue faide already that he is not

An abfolut Prince is not fubiecte vnto any ftranger.

subiect, or inferiour vnto any of his owne Nation: So is he neither to acknowledge any greater then him selfe abroade. Kinge EVMENES, though he was but a poore Prince, and had but one onely Castell of PERGAMON vnder his power: yet when he came to capitulating with ANTIGONVS the greate kinge of ASIA, he would not yeelde one iote vnto him in prerogatiue of honour: saying that, so long as he had his sworde by his side, he knew no man greater then him selfe: and yet by his leaue he fetched his fier from the Romanes, who mainteined him in all his quarrelles both against ANTIGONVS, and against PHILLIPPE kinge of MACEDONES. But our ROYALL Prince is not to shrewd him selfe vnder the shadow of an other, as EVMENES did vnder the Romanes: Nor to shield him selfe vnder any buckelar of Protection, as FERRARA doth vnder FRANCE: BOLOGNA vnder the POPE: FLORENCE and LVCCA vnder the kinge of SPAIGNE. Neither shall he paye tribute vnto any forreine Prince, as the Common weale of CARTHAGE, after it was subdued by SCIPIO AFRICANVS, did vnto the people of ROME. Neither yet any annuall pension is he to paye,

A Royall Prince needeth no Protection.

A Royall Prince is not tributarie vnto any.

as

Royall Monarchie. 47

as some great Princes of Christendome haue done vnto the greate Turke: The Common weales of VENICE, GENOVA, RAGVSA for the countreyes they haue confining vpon him doe yet the like. And as not long since LEWIS th'leuenth of FRANCE payed 50. thousand crownes a yeare vnto kinge HENRY the eight (of noble memorie) for to haue peace with him, and with our Nation. Much lesse shall he be Liege Vassall vnto any, as the kinges of SCOTLAND were wonte to be vnto the kinges of ENGLANDE: The Dukes of BRITANNIE vnto the kinges of FRANCE. Neither shall he holde in Fee, or Fealtie of any, as most of the Cities in ITALIE doe of th'Empire, and the kingdomes of NAPLES, and SICILLE doe of the Pope: The Knightes of MALTA of the kinge of SPAINE: these giuing yearly a Faulcon, those a white amblinge Geldinge, some one thing, some an other. VVhich all are certaine kindes of subiections, and spyces of Seruitude, carying with them a number of rightes, duties, honours, and reuerences, vnworthie of the dignitie of a ROYALL Prince. VVho must be as the Gramarians saye a Noune Substantiue able to stande of him selfe, without the

The most Royall Prince holdeth not in Fee or in Fealtie of any.

helpe, or aide of an other, without paying Tributes, doing Homages, swearing Fealties, and Loyalties vnto any forreine Prince. COSMVS Duke of FLORENCE (of late remembrance) might not be made kinge of TOSKANE, although Pope PIVS the fourth, had a good will to make him, Becauſe he helde his Cities, and Tounes of the Empire. VVherefore the Emperour hearing of his ſute: ſaide *Italia non habet Regem, niſi Cæſarem*. The French kinge FRANCES the firſt of that name, for to let CHARLES the fifth, as then Archeduke of AVSTRIA from being choſen Emperour, ſhewed vnto the Electours, how that the Imperiall Maieſtie ſhould be to much imbaſed, if they made of his vaſſall their chiefe, and Souueraigne. VVhich made the ſaide CHARLES hauing after taken FRANCES priſoner (at the famous battaile fought in the Parke of PAVIA) that he would neuer condeſcende vnto his deliuerance, vntill he was firſt exempted by FRANCES from all kinde of Seruices, and Subiections which he owed vnto the Crowne of FRANCE for the Countreyes he helde of ARTOYS and FLANDERS. It ſeemeth ſo baſe a thing vnto the Maieſtie of a ROYALL Prince, to become the Liege

Inconueniences proceding from Subiectios.

Royall Monarchie.   49

Liege man of an other: to sweare Fayth, and Loyaltie vnto an other: ioyning his handes within the handes of an other: to fall downe on his knees as TIRIDATES kinge of ARMENIA did before NERO: to kisse the Thresholde of the dore, as PRVSIAS kinge of BITHINIA did when he entered into the Senate house of ROME: to call him selfe the Seruant of an other, as ASDRVBALL called him selfe the FACTOR, and PROCVRATOR of the people of ROME: These (I saye) and such like Indignities proceeding from Protections, Tributes, Fealties, Loyalties, and the other kindes of the forenamed Subiections, are so much abhorring vnto the Soueraignitie of a ROYALL, and absolute Prince, as he will choose rather to parte from whole Countreyes, then to incurre, and indure such indignities. VVherefore quarells were made against the kinges of England (her MAIESTIES most ROYALL predecessours) touching the Dukedomes of GVYENNE, and NORMANDIE, The Earldome of POITOV, and MVTTRELL, and many other goodly Possessions, which they helde in FRANCE, because they vouchesaued not to be bounde to doe Honours, and Homages for the same.

Seruices annexed vnto the foresaide Subiectiōs.

G

But no meruaile though great kinges can not abide Subiections whē the Prince of ORANGE (this mans father) refused of the French kinge LEWIS th'eleuenth tenne times so much, as his Principallitie was worth, because he would not be subiecte to Seruices, and Vassallties. CALISTENES also the Nephew of ARISTOTLE, being but a priuate man, chose rather to dye, then he would (according to the maner of the Persians) fall downe prostrate and adore ALEXANDER, as a God aboue the estate of man. And I haue harde how an Imbassadour for the VENETIANS at CONSTANTINOPLE, when he was to haue audience of the Great TVRKE, vnto whome he coulde not haue accesse, but thorough a litle lowe place made of purpose, because men should come stoping, and kneeling vnto him: The VENETIAN Imbassadour, (supposing in him selfe the reuerend Hienesse of that estate,) creeped thorough the hole with his backe forewardes. A thing, which the GRAN SIGNOR can in no maner of waye abide to see a mans taile towardes him.

But for to retourne vnto our most ROYALL Prince, we will conclude that he is not to doe Homage, or Honour vnto any, not to paye Tribute,

bute, or Penſion vnto any, not to be ſubiect either at home, or abroade vnto any, not to holde in Fealtie, or in Loyaltie, by Protection, or by Commiſſion, nor for a ſhorte time or ſeaſon: But to rule really, fully, and perpetually, according as we haue in a generall maner hitherto diſcourſed. I coulde wiſhe to ſpeake more particularly of the ROYALTIES, and prerogatiues belonging vnto the Maieſtie of a Soueraine Prince: as of his power, and authoritie in allowing, and diſallowing of maters propounded to be Lawes: in proclaming of warres, and concluding of Peace: in chooſing, and refuſing of Magiſtrates: in coyning and rating of money: in erecting of Fortreſſes: in graunting Pardons, Licences, Liberties, and Priuileges: &c. But becauſe they are matters of more waight, and therefore doe require good aduiſement, and better authority: I thinke good to ſuſpende them vntill a more conuenient time, or elſe to commende them vnto thoſe, that are of more approued Iudgement, and better warranted to deale with them. In the meane while I hope, that theſe fewe lines of ours concerning the maner, and forme of the beſt Common weale, ſhall not ſeeme al-

Concluſion of the Treatice.

G ij

together impertinent to shew the Excellencie and Dignitie, the Power, and Maiestie of ROYALL MONARCHIE. VVhereby all good subiectes seeing the greatnesse which God hath indued Princes withall, to be as it were his LIEFTENANTES to gouerne vs here vppon Earth, may respecte, and reuerence them with all humilitie: Serue, and obaye them with all Loyaltie: heare, and speake of them with all honour.

T. V.

M. THOMAS NORTON
COVNSAILLER, AND SOL-
LICITER VNTO THE CITIE OF
London, hauing by th'appointement of the L. Bishop of London reade this Treatice and diligently perused the same, maketh this reporte therof vnto the Reader.

IN this booke, conferring therwith the protestation of the Gentleman the Autor therof, that he hath no other intent, but to geue signification of his deuotion, and duetyfulnesse to her *Maiestie*, as to the best Prince in the best forme of Estate, which I do *candidè* take to be the scope of his Treatie, I see nothing but that with good interpretation, hauing respect to the Authours good meaning, is in my opinion, and construction verie commendable, and safely to be reade to the honour of her *Maiestie*, & the incouraging of her *Maiesties* subiectes to acknowledge her Excellencie, to thanke God for her, and to yeelde her due obedience.

G iii

PROVERBI VVLGARI,
RACCOLTI IN DIVERSI
LVOGHI D'ITALIA, ET LA
maggior parte dalle proprie
bocche de gl' Ita-
liani steffi.

PER

*Carlo Merbury Gentil'huomo
Inglilese.*

ILQVALE NE FA PRESENTE
DI COSÌ FATTA SVA INDVSTRIA
à gl'amici, & patroni suoi honorati, della lingua Italiana
studiosi.

* *
*

A I NOBILI, ET ILLVSTRI SIGNORI DI CORTE, ET Altri gentil'huomini honorati, della lingua Italiana intendenti.

IO non sò (Signori Illustri) che luogo habbia trouato ne' vostri cortesi concetti quel mio precedente discorso: se riguardando all' altezza del suo suggetto, voi desiderate in me maggior isperienza, e più gagliardo giudicio: ò se considerando la fine, & l'intentione di quello, vi contentiate della mia debita, quantunque debole industria. La mia isperienza io confesso veramente esser picciolissima, sì come di persona poco prattica nelle cose de gli stati: & quanto àl mio giudicio, non mene attribuisco punto; conoscendomi giouane di poche lettere, & di men che mezzano ingegno. Mà purè, poi ch'io mi son ingegnato d'ingagliardire, & quella, & questo, & tutte l'altre forze mie col desiderio di mostrar la mia debita diuotione verso il felicissimo stato della nostra Serenissima Principessa: Io spero, che voi Signori di Corte (I quali viuete nella viua & continua contemplatione di quella sua Maestà, in honor & riuerenza di cui tendono quelli pensieri, &

& difcorfi miei) fpero dico, & quafi m'afficuro, che voi vi contentarete di fauorir à così fatta mia imprefa: non mirando già tanto alla dignità di quella (troppo alta per l'ale mie,) nè alla fua difficultà (troppo pefante per le fpalle mie,) mà alla diligenza, ftudio, induftria, & al buon animo mio: di che fe ben altro effetto non ne fegue, nè altro vtile non rifulta al lettore (& pure non tengo lo trattato fia con modeftia detto, affatto inutile,) ch'vna nuda fignificatione della mia viua voglia: non è però, che la buona mente nõ fia da Dio attefa, & da voi tenuta in conto. Vi fi prefenta ancora vn' altro parto della mia induftria, il quale poi che non è mio figliuolo naturale, ma adottiuo, & d'altre lingue che della mia leccato, (fe ben uon d'altra mano, che dalla mia raccolto, veftito, & prodotto in quefta luce) più arditamente velo raccommando: afficurandoui, che fe vi degnate d'vfarlo, & d'adoperarlo, egli vi farà di molti, & molti fegnalati feruitij. Egli vi moftrerà creanze & vfanze foreftiere: vi darà ammaeftramenti al viuer vtili, auertimenti al conuerfar conueneuoli: fe v'occorre vfar ragionamento famigliare, egli vi farà à canto: fe pùr v'accade entrar in qualche difcorfo graue, egli farà là anche prefente, fempre miniftrandoui qualche bel motto, ò qualche bel detto per confirmar le voftre ragioni. Per conto poi di quella lingua, della quale voi (Signori, & gentil'huomini giouani, al cui feruitio l'ho fpetialmente indrizzato) vi delettate; non vi poffo dire, quanto honoreuol àiuto (fe lo trattenete bene) vene potrà auuenire. Voi fapete, ch' in ogni lingua non c'è più bella gratia, che l'vfar, & nel parlare, & nel fcriuere, dì bei, & fpeffi Prouerbi: I quali, sì per le fcelte, & purgate parole, che vi fi trouano; fi per le belle metafore, & allegorie delle quali per lo più fi
com-

compongono, per l'acutezza che vi si scuopre, recondita & non cosi nota, come quella fauella che s'vsa ordinariamente parlando; come ancora perche sono quasi voci diuine riceuuti, & per commun consenso da tutti approuati:par che portino seco(non sò come) vna certa authorità, dignità, & Maestà à quel che si scriue, & si dice. Di così fatti Prouerbi questo vostro Italico seruitore vi fornirà à pieno nella sua lingua volgare, prestandouene tanti, & tanti, che se degnate à mandarne solamente la minore, ò la migliore parte alla vostra memoria (sì come il suo primo patrone altre volte n'ha mandato la maggiore,& non se n'è pentito, anzi sen' è seruito pùr assai,)Vedrete, che vi correranno per ogni verso leggiadri & vaghi Prouerbi, sentenze illustri & celebrate, belle parole & purgate, motti Toscani, modi Italiani: in maniera che di sì fatta forte in breue spatio vi s'auanzerà la lingua, si purgeranno le parole, vi si crescerà la creanza, s'arricchera il giudicio, & tutti insieme sì realmente in voi s'incorporeranno, che parerà ch' in vn subito voi vi siate trasferiti in Italia, & d'Italia ritornati senza passar ò mare, ò monti. A me veramente Signori essendo in Italia, mi è riuscito tanto dà valent' huomo questo vostro seruitore (che più non lo chiamo mio, ma vostro hauendolo raccommandato à voi) & mi son tanto ben seruito & sodisfatto dell' opera sua, che s'io ho mai fatto qualche progresso nella lingua Toscana, lo debbo certò in gran parte riconoscere da lui. Le cose sue sono brieui à ricordare: facili ad intendere, (sì l'ho facilitate io ancora, doue m' è parso bisogno:) argute & piaceuoli per dilettare: sono varie, raccolte non in Siena, ò in Fiorenza solò, ma in diuersi & diuersi altri luoghi d'Italia: sono anche Rare per non esser già tanto d'ogni scrittore frequentate, quanto solamente per le bocche de gl' huomini in commũ parlar vsate; non gia tutte fuor da libri cauate, ma la maggior parte dalle proprie mani de gli Italiani stessi riceuute. Vi debbono anche questi Prouerbi esser via più grati, perche hauendo essi fatti molti viaggi meco, & corsi per mare & per terra molti pericoli; par che siano stati da qualche gratia diuina à posta riserbati, per farne presente a i vostri honorati studi; a i quali mille volte li raccommando, basciandoui le mani.

❈ ❈
❈

VARIA COLLETTIONE
DI PROVERBI VVLGA-
RI, SENTENZE ILLVSTRI,
DETTI BREVI, ET VAGHI MOTTI,
che s'vsano nella lingua Italiana, copiosissima,
& felicissima in così fatte cose, massi-
me nel Prouerbiare.

L'HVOMO *propone, & Dio dispone.*
Quel ch' e disposto in Cielo, bisogna che sia.
Accasca in vn punto quel, che non accasca in cent' anni.
Bisogna quando altri è*incudine, soffrire: quando*martello, percuotere.   * An anuyle. *A hammer.
Egl' è mal boccone, quel ch' affoga.
Beato colui, chi puo far beato altrui.
La necessità non hà legge.
Chi serue, & tace, assai dimanda.
Che premio mio piace al ben seruire, pur viene al fine, se ben tarda à venire.
Il mal non stà sempre, doue si pone.
Sono caduto dalla*padella (come dice il vulgo) nelle*brage, cio è da mal in peggio.   *Frying Pan. x Burning coales.
Facilmente si truoua il bastone per dar il cane.
Bisogna legar l'asino, doue vuole il patrone.
Le disgratie non vadano mai scompagniate.
I sogni non son veri, & i disegni non riescono.
Chi mal pensa, mal dispensa.

Trouble.	Chi cerca *briga, la troua à sua posta.
	Però non cercar quel che non ti tocca.
	Chi potendo stare, cade tra via, s'ei rompe il collo, suo danno.
	Il mondo è tondo, & dopo la notte vien il giorno: & ogni tempo vien, à chi lo può aspettare.
	Più sa il matto in casa sua, ch'il sauio in quella d'altri.
	Il ben non fu mai tardi.
	Chi nasce matto, non guarisce mai.
Scrape.	Chi di gallina nasce conuien che *razzoli.
	Chi si contenta, gode.
Beraieth, or defileth him selfe.	Chi si loda, * s'imbroda.
	Tutto quello che riluce, non è oro.
Pillow, or bolsterre.	Che profitta, rauedersi dopo il fatto, ò tardare à pentirsi al *capezzale.
	Se s'auesse à fare la cosa due volte, ciascuno sarebbe sauio.
	Chi hà tempo non aspetti tempo, ma pigli' il bene, quando viene.
	Ch' il mondo è fatto à scale, chi le scende, chi le sale: & l'hore non tornano à dietro.
	In una vernata sola gli alberi mutano faccia, & il giudicar il presente per il passato non è sempre sicuro.
	Meglio è rauedersi una volta, che non mai.
	Però chi non hà ceruello habbia gambe: si suol dire, quando un s'è scordato d'una cosa, & gli bisogna tornar in dietro.
	Il peggior di tutti i peccati, è l'ostinatione.
The handle.	Gl' è un gittar il *manico dietro alla palla.
	I gattucci hanno aperti gli occhi.
Shroutyde.	Al * carnouale si conosce chi hà la gallina grassa.
	Io conosco i miei polli al raspiare.
To bray like an Asse.	Al *ragghiare si vedrà, che non è Leone.
	Chi più hà, più s'imbratta.
	Chi Asino è, & ceruio esser si crede, al saltar di fossa se n'auede.

Non

VOLGARI.

Non è ben sempre dir il tutto, anzi dicono, è meglio mangiar quel, ch' altri hà, che dir quel, che altri sà.
In bocca serrata non entrò mai mosca.
Però si dice tien la lingua fra i denti.
La lingua non hà osso, ma fà rompere il dosso.
Le funi legano i buoi, & le parole gli huomini.
Chi troppo parla, spesso falla.
Si dice ancora che chi troppo parla è tenuto matto,
Et chi non parla diuien muto affatto.
E sauiezza parlar poco, & ascoltar assai.
Vn par d'orecchie seccano cento lingue.
La lingua corre, doue il dente duole.
Chi non parla, Dio non l'ode.
Et però di il fatto tuo, & lascia fare al diauolo.
Il vitio di contradire è proprio de gli insensati. — Prouerbio antico.
Costui vuol toccare il cielo con vn dito, cioè, è glorioso.
A cader và, chi troppo in alto sale.
Non vanno si alte l'ale mie.
Si lascia taluolta la carne per l'ombra. — As we saye, Selfe doe, selfe haue.
*Qual Asino dà in parete, tal riceue.
Chi dorme co' cani, si leua con le *pulci. — * Flease.
* Stuzzicare il * vespaio, è cosa pericolosa. — To play, or touche wantonly. A waspes neste.
Chi schernisce il * Zoppo, dè esser diritto.
Tutte le cose vbidiscono al danaio. — A lame man
Io veggo, che secondo il prouerbio. Volete star lontan da Gioue & dal Folgore : cio è fuor d'ogni pericolo al sicuro.
A' i molini, & alle donne sempre manca qualche cosa : cio è alle donne troppo curiose. — Stakes, or postes.
I panni rifanno le * stanghe.
Vestì vn bastone, & parrà vn barrone.
Può sostenere il Toro, chi haurà già portato il vitello.
Chi non s'arrischia, non guadagna.

Chi vuol del pesce, bisogna che s'imbratti, & s'immolli le brache.

Egl'è difficilissimo andar à veder macinare, senza imbiancarsi di farina.

Non vien un male, che non vien per bene.

Prou.Sanese. *Chi pecora si fa, il lupo se lo mangia.*

Che si perde multo per esser stolto.

Is fleade. *Alla pruoua si * scortica l'asino: & molte cose son meglio crederle, che prouarle.*

Bisogna tal volta pena patire, per bella parere.

Se io hò delle corna in seno, non me le voglio metter in capo.

Perche è mala cosa esser cattiuo, ma egl'è peggior l'esser conosciuto.

E buona cosa esser lodato, ma è meglior il meritarlo.

Chi há poca vergogna, tutt'il mondo è suo.

Barketh. *Il can, che vuol mordere non * abbaia.*

Et doue bisognano i fatti, le parole sono d'auanzo.

Dal detto al fatto v'e un'gran tratto.

Chi non fa, men falla.

Moate. *Mira la * bruscha d'altri, & non vede la sua traue.*

Chi há bocca vuol mangiare.

La commoditá fa l'huomo ladro.

All'arca aperta il giusto pecca.

Cricket. *Ogni * grillo grilla à sé.*

Scrapeth. *Ogni gallo * ruspa á sé.*

Et ogni un tira l'acqua al suo molino.

Prou.Sanese. *La girlauda ancor che costi un quatrino, la non sta bene in capo ad ogni uno.*

Quel è tuo nimico, chi è del tuo officio.

Fra Corsali, & Corsali non si perde che barili voti.

Fra barcaiuolo, & marinaio non si quadagna se non cose da ferro vecchio.

Non fu mai un si tristo, che si nõ trouasse un perggior di lui.

Perche

VOLGARI.

Perche ogni diritto hà il suo rouerscio.
E mal sordo, quel che non vuol vdire.
Fallo celato è mezzo perdonato.
Cagna frettolosa fà i cagnuoli ciechi.
Non si fé mai nulla bene in fretta, se non il fuggir la peste.
D'Eforo sete diuenuto Teopompo, de' quali quello haueua bisogno di sprone questo di freno.
Chi guarda ad ogni penna, non fà mai letto.
Fà d'vna mosca, vn Elefante.
Tre donne fanno vn mercato, cio è donne parlatrice.
Egli è vn sparger le perle fra i porci.
Stamo in Casa Talpa, & fuori Argo: cio è veggiamo molto di lontano, & nulla d'appresso.
Mescolar zucche con lanterne: come à dire parole Lombarde con Toscane.
Troppo veramente s'arischia, chi del proprio giudicio s'assicura.
Et è volgar detto, che àl ben s'appiglia, chi ben si consiglia.
Dimmi con cui tù vai, & saprò quel che fai.
*Vi sono di quelli, che secondo il prouerbio hanno il mele in bocca e 'l * rasato à cintola.*   * A Raiser as his Girdle.
A can mansueto il lupo par feroce, & la virtù va à terra senza la confidenza.
Si dice ch' il nobil ama, e 'l villan teme.
Del rio seruo peggior parte è la lingua.
Tant' nimici habbiamo, quanti seruitori : vero è, se non sono fideli.
Gli par sempre di mangiar il cascio nella trapola: cio è à chi stà in prigione.
Hà consumato più olio, che vino: si dice d'vn huomo studioso.
La verità è nel vino.
La fiamma è poco lontana dal fumo.

Amor vuol fede, & fede vuole fermezza.

Aqua lontana non spegne fuoco vicino: s'intende d'vn rimedio tardo.

Grasso ventre non genera sottil ingegno.

E mala cosa lisciar il pelo ál seruitore: cio è lodarlo, o adulardo.

Punge il villan, chi l'vnge: vnge, ch'il punge.

Tale è la cagnuola, quale è la Signora.

Quale è il padre tal sono i figliuoli.

Qual é il Rettore, tal sono i popoli.

Il pesce commincia à putir dal capo: cio è I vitij de' seruitori hanno ad esser ascritti al patrone.

Buon cauallo, ò mal cauallo vuol sperone.

Dal mattino si conosce il buon giorno.

Si suole dire, che chi hà cauallo bianco, & bella moglie, non é mai senza doglie.

Non é bestia più pazza di quella del popolo, né acqua più grossa di quella del *macheroni.

*A certaine kinde of past boiled, and made as it were in fritters to be eaten.

Dio mi guardi da due cose: l'vna da' segnati da Dio, l'altra dall'acque quiete.

Dio mi guardi da hoste nuouo, & puttana vecchia.

Ogni vn conta della fiera, come egli andò con essa.

Talhor per vn brutto viso, si perde vna buona compagnia.

Porco pigro non mangiò mai pera mezza.

Cinqu'hore dorme il viandante: sette il studiante: & vndeci ogni forfante.

I dispetti, & i rispetti guastano il mondo.

Tanto é il bene che non gioua, quanto il mal che non nuoce.

Chi non vuol ballare, non vadi al ballo, perche poi ehe altri é dentro, bisogna ballare.

Contra due non la potrebbe Orlando.

Chi la vorrà solo dunque contra due Orlandi?

Vien l'asino di montagna, & caccia il caual di stalla.

Al

VOLGARI.

*Al tutto è * orbo, chi non vede il sole.*   *Blinde.
La paura guarda la vigna.
Stiedi, & gambetta, & vedrai tua vendetta.
Quel imboccarsi per man d'altri, è vn non sattolarsi mai.
Chi ti fá più carezze, che non suole, ò t'hà ingannato, ò ingannarti vuole: altri dicono, ò ingannar, ò tradir ti vuole.
Le galline si pigliano con belle belle, non con scioia, scioia.
*Tal mano si bascia, che si vorrebbe veder * mozza.*   *Cut of.
Non è ingannato, se non chi si fida.
Ogni bel giuoco, rincresce.
Ben spesso si piglia delle volpe.
*Non è miglior Rimedio che tener lungi dal * becco l'herba,*   *A Goate.
& far discostar le serue dal marito.
Egli é meglio esser Martire, che confessore.
Picciola pioggia fá cessar gran vento: s'intende delle lagrime di donne.
*Il spensierato fa come il Magnano, che salta tanto con le * bolge, come senza le bolge.*   *Budgettes.
Onde dice il volgo: Il saper nulla, è vna dolce vita.
Per far buon giudicio del vino, bisogna dar prima colore à gli occhi, dapoi l'odore al naso, & finalmente il sapore alla bocca.
Non si vuol tagliar il fuoco col ferro: cio è non contendere co' contentiosi.
Hà la fame più grande, che il ventre.
Da ventre pieno esce miglior consiglio: cio è più fidele, & manco astuto.
E meglio esser sol, che mal accompagnato.
La compagnia nel male suole allegierir il male.
Io non vorrei esser solo in paradiso.
Le pietre, che vanno rotolando, non piglian rugine.
Il seruitore dé ò seruir, come seruo, ò fuggir come ceruo.

I iij

Há talmente dalla crapula ingrossato l'intelletto, che non conosce (secondo il Prouerbio) la traggea dalla *Gragnuola: & gl'è giuditioso, come l'asmo che giudicò più soaue il canto del cucco, che quello del * Rosignuolo.

* Haile, or yce.
* A nightingall.

Quando la Patrona solleggia, la fante dannegia.

* to whistle.

Non si può insieme bere, & *fischiare,
Chi non fá quel che deue, quel che aspetta non riceue.
Et altri dicono: Chi non fa quel che debbe, gli interuien quel che non crede.
Quando il Marito fá terra, la moglie fá carne: s'intende della moglie cattiua, & disleale.
Vá circando il pelo nel' ouo.
La lettera non s'arrossisce, né si vergogna.
La verità si può piegare, ma rompere non giá mai.
Chi è facile à credere, si troua ingannato spesso.
Si grida poche volte ál lupo, che non sia in paese.
Il villano vien sempre col disegno fatto.
Tal ti guarda la cappa, che non ti vede la borsa.
Non é peccato ál mondo si manifesto, che non si venga à manifestare.
Però diceua la fornaia, se non vuoi, che si sappia, non lo fare, & se vuoi tenerlo secreto, non lo dire.
Chi non sa tacere, non sa godere.
Chi há intrigato ista cosa, la strighi: chi há mangiato i * baccelli, spazzi i gusci.

*new beanes

Chi vá alle nozze, & non é inuitato, spesso se ne torna suergognato.
Chi scriue à chi non risponde, ò l'è matto, ò l'há di bisogno.
Di promesse non godere, & di minaccie non temere.
Amor, & Signoria non voglion compagnia.
Chi biasima vuol comprare.
Mangiati à tuo modo, ma vestiti à modo d'altri.
Chiunque ad altrui inganni tesse, in se stesso non poco
mal

VOLGARI.

mal ordisce.

Ode, vede, & tace, se vuoi viuere in pace.

Carne fá carne, vino fá sangue: pan mantiene.

Dio mi guardi dalle mattutine di Parigi, & le vespre di Sicilia.

Bologna la grassa, Padoua la passa, ma Venetia la guasta.

Chi vuole del fresco, non vadi à cercarlo.

Tien coperta la testa nel giorno manco che puoi, & nella notte quanto che vuoi.

Conti spessi fanno amicitie lunghe.

Chi fá la sua vendetta, oltre che offende,
Chi offeso l'há, da molti si defende.

Chi più spende, manco spende.

Spesso vna molestia ne leua molte.

Il fuoco arde la * paglia facilmente.   *Strawe.

Cosa, che voglia cadere, fá prima cenno.

In vn buon seruitore ci vuole il muso di Porco, la schiena d'Asino, & le gambe di Ceruo.

Spesse volte il giorno d'oggi aggiugne qualche cosa à quello d'hieri.

Chi si marita in fretta, se ne pente adagio.

Pigliar vna donna brutta, è mal di stomacho,
Pigliarla bella è mal di testa.

Questo è come * pestoiar acqua nel * Mortaio, ò gittar le   *To stomp
   * Faue al muro, & come perdere l'acqua, el' sapone.   * Morter.
     * Beanes.

Chi hauendo tempo, aspetta tempo, tempo perde.

Con il tempo, & con la paglia si maturano le nespole.

Il più delle volte auiene, che la maggior parte vince la migliore.

I vecchi, che schirzano con le donne fanno carezze alla morte.

A buono Intendimento non bisogna molte parole.

La scusa non richiesta, presuppone errore.

D'un errore sempre ne nascono altri maggiori.
La fuga si fà tarda, per troppo spronare.
Vien la vernata, che ne và l'agnel prima, che la capra.
Chi fà i fatti suoi, non s'imbrata le mani.
Chi non sa fare i fatti suoi, peggio fa quei d'altri.
Quel ch'è del patto, non è d'inganno.
I monti firmi stanno, mà gl' huomini à rincontrarsi si vanno
La facilità non impedisce l'elegantia.
Chi lascia la via vecchia per la nuoua, spesso ingannato si truoua.
Caual donato non si guarda in bocca.
Né femina, né tela non pigliar alla candela : s'intende delle donne che si lisciano.
Assai sà, chi non sà, se tacer sà.
Se non con la pelle del Leone, con la pelle della volpe.
La conscienza è mille testimonij.
La marauiglia è figliuola della ignoranza.
Vn huomo val cento, & cento non val vno.
Chi semina virtù, raccoglie fama.
L'vna mano laua l'altra, & ambedue lauano il viso.
Bocca larga : borsa stretta.
Mentre che v'è acqua, bisogna molinare, & mentre è caldo, battere.
Ciascuno Molino resta di molinare mancando l'acqua.
Chi comporta vn ingiuria vecchia inuita altrui à fargli vn' altra nuoua.

Prouerbio Bolognese.
Putto in vin, & donna in Latin, non fecer mai buon fin.
Fra sepolto Tesoro, & occulta sapienza, non si conosce alcuna differenza.
Seruo d'altrui si fà, chi dice il suo secreto, à chi no'l sà.
L'adulatore è simile al beccaio, che grata il porco con la mano, per dargli poi della mazza sù'l capo.
Chi vuol entrare, piccij l'vscio.

Più

VOLGARI. 17

Il diauolo non è si brutto, come si depinge.
Il diauolo sá, perche è vecchio.
A cane, che lecca cenere, è mal fidarli la farina.
Al can che fiuta farina, si può ben fidar cenere.
*Quel sarebbe come porre il Lupo per * pecoraio, & andar*   * A sheepe-
   alla gatta per lardo.   hearde.
Né Christo ancora si potè guardare da man di traditore.
Legalo bene, & lascialo andare.
Piscia chiaro, & fà le fiche ál medico.
Io leuai la lepre, & vn' altro la prese.
Al' arbore che cade, ogniun grida taglia taglia, & al can che
   fugge dágli dágli.
Ogn' vn corre à far legna al arbore, ch' il vento in terra
   getta.
Dio mi guardi da furia di populo, da cattiua giustitia, & da
   man di traditori.
Non è in tutto sauio, chi non sà bisognando esser pazzo.
La gatta há pelata la coda.
Chi altri tribola, se non posa.
Andarono per sonare, & furono sonati : come i piffari di Prouerbio
   Lucca.   Lucchese.
Chi tutto vuole, tutto perde.
Chi ben siede, mal pensa.
Tal biasima altrui, che tira à ` suoi colombi.
Accennaua à coppe & daua bastoni.
Non è peggior male, che quel della morte : nè peggior mine-
   stra, che quella che sá del fumo.
L'amore, & la tosse non si ponno celare.
Non si serra mai vna porta, che non si apra vn' altra.
Loda, & comforta, & non t'obligare.
Sempre de' cattiui partiti, piglia il migliore.
Però si dice in Italia che per arte, & inganno si viue il mez-
   zo anno: per inganno & arte si viue l'altra parte.

                                                              K

Alla buona diratapensauisu.
Non sono tutti huomini, quelli che pisciano al muro.
Bisogna gustar il mele con la punta delle dita: cio è vsar vna cosa non per cibo ordinario, ma come per ristoratiuo.
L'aquila non piglia le mosche.
L'infelici figliuoli lodano i padri: volendo dire ch'essi stessi son d'ogni lode indegni.
Questo non sarebbe altro, che voler torre il folgore à Gioue: ò entrare in altrui possessione.
L'ingannar se stesso è la più facil cosa di tutte l'altre.
I secondi pensieri son sempre migliori.
Chi falla la seconda, tocca vn cauallo.
Par vn Toscano di Monferrato: Si dice d'vno ch'è troppo curioso nel parlare.
L'agnello humile succia le mamelle della propria madre, & l'altre ancora.
Da mal Coruo, mal ouo.
Le donne s'hanno à sposare prima con l'orecchie, che con gli occhi.
Voi volete dire, ch' io imbocco (secondo il Prouerbio) col

* with an empty spone *cucchiaio voto*: cio è mostro di voler fare, & non fare.
E meglio pascer febre, che pascer debolezza: volendo dire, che l'infermità, che vengono da repletione sono menò pericolose, che quelle, che procedono da estenuatione.

The Rudder of a boate. *Il vino non há* * *timone.*
L'è vn voler estinguer il fuoco con l'oglio,
Picciol vento accende fuoco, ma vn grande l'estingue.

* Caakes. *M' hauete renduto pan per* * *foccacia.*
Più dolci sono le ferite del amico, ch' i baci del inimico.
Le cose malamente acquistate, malamente se ne vanno.
Vn bel morir tutta la vita honora.

Freno

VOLGARI. 19

Freno indorato non migliora il cauallo.
Se l'occhio non mira, il cuor non sospira.
Che quanto piace al mondo è breue sogno.
Chi porta il torchio indietro há per costume,
 à se far ombra, à chi lo segue lume.
Non shirzar che doglia, non motteggiar del vero.
Gli huomini da bene sono sì pochi, che si posson numerare
 col' Naso.
Lodando il buono, è poi sempre migliore,
Riprendi il tristo, ogn' hora ne vien peggiore.
Chi dice tutto quel ch' egli sà, fà tutto quel ch' egli può, &
 mangia cio ch' egli hà, non gli resta più niente.
Con l'ombra della virtù si depinge il vitio,
Et sotto il conio della bontà si spende la malitia.
*Egl' è formica di sorbo, che non esce per * bussare.*   * to knocke.
Bisogna esser tagliato a buona Luna.
Ogni cosa ha principio.
Muro bianco carta da matti.
Per via s'acconciano le Some.
Egli scorticarebbe il pedocchio per hauer la pelle.
Quanto vno ha più roba, tanto più ne vorrebbe hauere.
Há fatto più che Carlo in Francia: cio è cose incredibili.
Tristo è colui ch' aspetta la mercè d'altrui.
L'auaro inanzi ch' egli scōdesse il Tesoro, perse se medesimo.   Sent.
Tanto gode l'auaro hauendo nulla, quanto hauendo ogni cosa.
I danari non statiano l'auaro, ma gli fanno hauere più sete
 di quelli.
L'huomo virtuoso ama più d'essere, che d'esser tenuto.
La spada de' tristi non taglia, ma il credito de' buoni amaz-
 za l'huomo.
Chi si becca il ceruello in vn modo, chi in vn altro.
S'io trouassi l'inimico à dormire, non gli torcerei vn pelo.
Vn pazzo ne fa cento.

          K ij

Il scriuitor i sciocco suol esser spesse volte nel rubare astuto.
I bnoni costumi si debbono honorare non meno ch' i capei ca-
                    (nuti.
*Bemyreth.   L'amore *infanga il giouane, & il vecchio *annega.
*Drouneth.   Non desideri mai nissuno d'esser il primo à portar cattiua
    nouella.
    Quel che tu vuoi donare vna volta, non lo prometter due.
    Non sa donare chi tarda à dare.
    La legge poche volte resiste ál Oro.
*Breaketh in   Il martell d'argento *spezza le porte di ferro.
peeces.   A far bene le facende, bisogna ben pensare, meglio consiglia-
    re, ottimamente deliberare, & perfettamente fare.
    Il pouero s'affattica in cercar quello che gli manca, il ricco in
    conseruar quello ch'egl' ha, & il virtuoso nel domandar
    quel' che gli bisogna.
*A greene   Ei fu buon * Papero, & cattiua ocha: cio è fu miglior mas-
goose.   saio in giouentù, che in vecchiezza, meglio com-
    portana la pouertà che la ricchezza.
    Virtù è, fuggir il vitio.
    Chi non fa le pazzie in giouentù le fa poi in vecchiezza.
    L'oro s'esperimenta col fuoco, con il martello si pruoua l'ar-
    gento, & con l'adoperare si conoscono gl' huomini.
*that kreakes   La più cattiua Ruota del carro è quella che * cigoli.
    Chi cerca i fatti d'altri non puo esser buona.
Sent.   Ogni ignorante è cattiuo.
    L'arbor buono fa buon frutto.
*Pawe.   Tanto và là gatta ál Lardo, che vi lascia la * zampa.
* Cawderne.   La padella dice al* Paiuolo, fatti in la che tu mi tingi: si puo
    vsar questo Prouerbio, per raffar i maledicenti.
    Ama è serai amato.
Sent. di Pla-   Amore è il vero prezzo con che si compra l'Amore.
tone.   Ogn' vn s'il becca: si dice propriamente de' poeti.
* Steele.   Tutto * l'acciaio ch' egli hà adosso non potrebbe fare vna
    punta d'vn ago.

                      Non

VOLGARI. 21

*Non si può trar la * ranocchia dal * Pantano.*   *Frogge.
*Chi laua il capo al Asino perde il * ranno, el' sapone.*   *Myre.
Tal merito ha, chi ingrato serue.   *Lee.
Di buon seme mal frutto.
Il sapere hà vn piede in terra & vno in Naue, Perche Si-
   gnoreggia l'acqua & la terra.
*Tu hai fatto d'vna lanza vn * fuso. cio è pensando d'esser*   *Spindle.
   Gigante nel sapere, ti sei mostrato vn Pigmeo.*
Impacciati co' fanti,
Et lascia stare i Santi.
*Tu sei fatto come la * Castagna,*   * A chesnut.
*Bella di fuori, & dentro è la * magagna.*   * A magott.
Si vuol andar col pie del piombo.
Non ti conosco, se non ti maneggio.
Duro con duro non fece mai buon Muro.
*Non si può distendersi, che quanto è lungo il * linzuolo.*   * Sheete.
Chi ha moglie ha pena & doglie: s'intende della cattiua.
*Egli ha tolto vn * sonaglio per vn * anguinaia.*   * A hawkes bell.
Chi non può battere il cauallo, batte la sella.   *Byle.
Io leuai la lepre vn' altro la prese.
Chi fa la roba non la gode.
*Nido fatto * gazza morta.*   † A birde called a Pye.
* *L'huomo honora il luogo, & non il luogo l'huomo.*
Le parole son femine, & i fatti son maschi.   *Detto di Cicerone.
Predica il Vangelo ad altri, & egli non crede nulla.
Costui sene và alla Carlona : cio è alla libera.
*Fà come il * Papagallo, che non leua mai il piede, se non ha*   *A popiniaye
   *prima appiccato il * becco :* cio è non scriue ne serue   * Bill.
   se non sia prima premiato.
Andò aggirando vn pezzo, come mosca senza capo.
Fa come le capre che saltan tutte doue ne salta vna.
Buone parole, & cattiui fatti ingannano i sauij & i matti.
Ciascun Molino resta di molinare, mancando l'acqua.

                            K iij

* A Thorne.	Vuol fare d'un * Pruno un * Melarancio.
* An Orége.	La campana suona per altri, & non per se.
	Fa come la candela: è buono à gli altri & à se medissimo fa
	Egli è meglio un tieni tieni, che cēto piglia piglia. (danno.
* A Crabbe.	Il sauio ben spesso caua'l * Grancio dalla * buca con la mano
* A Hole.	Vuol pigliar la Lepre con il carro. (d'altri.
	Egli è sauio dopo il fatto.
Sent.	Nō per passar il tēpo ma per acquistar tēpo si leggono i libri.

Più tosto si dé guardare dell' inuidia del Amico, che dall
 insidie del nimico.
Non conosce la pace, & non la stima,
Chi non hà prouato la guerra prima.
Il cane abbaia, doue si pasce.
Ogni cane vuol pisciar al muro.
Ogni tristo cane mena la coda.
Il far il letto al cane è gran fatica.
La fiamma è poco lontana dal fumo.
Nelle guerre d'Amore chi fugge, vince.
Lo faremo credere ancho à San Thomaso.
Quando l'oro parla, la lingua non ha forza alcuna.
Chi hà Amore in seno, ha sempre le sprone al fianco.
Chi scampa d'un punto ne scifa mille.
Da un lato hò il precipitio, & dall'altro i lupi.
Si vuol amar amico col suo difetto.
Dire villania al surdo, & scolparsi sopra la fortuna, sono
 cose d'huomini dappoco.
E più facil cosa tener un carbone ardente, che una secreta
 parola in bocca.
Il perder fá mal sangue: Giocar & perder lo sá far ogni uno.
La moscha ha la sua colera, & non è si picciol pelo che non
 habbia la sua ombra.
Non bisogna stuzzicare, quando fuma il naso del orso.
Ogni mal fresco ageuolmente si leua.

Non è buona madre quella, che fà il figliuolo, & non hà poi latte di poterlo nutrire.
E meglio perdere dicendo il vero, che vincer con le bugie.
Non può il vitello, & vuol che porti il bue.
Costui vuol abbracciar l'ombra, & pigliar il vēto con le reti.
Fà come il gallo, che canta bene, ma creſpa male: cio è ha buone parole ma cattiui fatti.
Colui và in *zoccoli per l'asciuto: cio è si dà fastidio senza cagione.   * Slippers.
Chi ben dona, caro vende, se villan non è ch' il prende.
L'huomo è dio al huomo, & Lupo.
Non bisogna per gli uccelli restar di seminare il grano.
Ogni * cuffia lorda serue per la notte.   *Euery fowle coyfe.
Non si crede al bugiardo, anco che giuri.
Ben si crede al verace, anchor che menta.
Più scende, chi più sale.
A sciascuno passo nasce un pensier nuouo.
Il serpente tra fiori, & herbe giace.
E tempo à cenare à i ricchi quando vogliono, & à i poueri
La gola non ha orecchie.   *(quando possono.*
La Salimanda uon è offesa dal fuoco.
Il medico è grasso, e'l religioso è magro.
Io chi sono di cera al fuoco torno.
L'aquila non genera colombe.
Vn tacer à tempo auanza ogni bel parlare.
Si vuol saper con i più, & parlar can i manco.
Merita ogni biasimo quel giouane che vuol parlar come vec- Sent. *chio, & quella donna che vuol parlare come huomo.*
In giouenil fallire è men vergogna: dice il Poeta.
Tre sorte di persone odiose al mondo. vz. Il pouero superbo: Il ricco bugiardo: E'l vecchio stolto.
L'esser canuto è segno di tempo, ma non di sapere.
Doue è manco cuore, quiui è più lingua.

Tanto più manifestasi il peccato,
Quanto più il peccator é in alto stato.
Chi riceue beneficio per via di prieghe, lo compra caro.
Chi viue per altrui, é morto in se stesso.
Val più vn' vncia di fortuna, che cento pesi d'industria.
E molto meglio meritar vn honore che hauerlo.
Perdonando troppo à chi falla, si fa ingiuria à chi non falla.
    del Cortegiano.
E peggio non voler far bene, che non saperlo fare.

Sent.   *La misura del hauere debb' esser il corpo del huomo: si come*
    il piede é la misura della scarpa.
La pace non armata é debole.
La diffidenza é la radice di sapienza.
Il magistrato fa manifesto il valor di chi l'essercita. del
Chi si contenta, gode.   (Guicciardini.
Chi fa la casa in piazza vn dice ch' ella é alta, & l'altro
    ch' ella é bassa.
La verità si può piegare, ma rompere non giamai.
Senza oro & argento non s'entra dentro.
Ira senza forza é cosa vana.
Ad amor palese rare volte é cōceduto felice fine. del Bocca.
Tra felici, & infelici nel mezzo della lor vita non v' é dif-
    ferenza alcuna.
Donna basciata, & mezzo guadagnata.
Sola la miseria é senza inuidia nelle cose presenti.
Per vna percossa non cadde mai arbore.
Le puttane sono come il carbone, che, ò coce, ò tinge.
Chi vuol esser ricco ageuolmente, hòr sia pouero di desi-
    derij. disse Cleante.

* Haie.   *Non é più tempo à dar* * *fieno à* * *oche.*
* Geese.
La vita fugge, & non s'arresta vn' hora,
    Et la morte vien dietro à gran giornate.
La vita il fine, e'l di loda la sera.
                                        Trotto

Trotto d'Asino dura poco.
Vn fior non fá Primauera.
Chi dona al indegno, due volte perde.
Non é bel quel ch' é bello,
Ma bello é quel che piace.
Chi dà tosto dà due volte.
Al Bugiardo non é creduto la verità.
Pensa & poi fa. Da & poi di.
Chi vno ne castiga cento ne minaccia.   Detto di Seneca.
Sarebbe troppo per vn cauallo, & poco per vn carro.
Ogni vn chi sta male desidera ruina.
Egli ha fatto il suo de * ruffola, * raffola.   *Thinges pilfered.
Dal detto àl fatto v' é vn gran tratto.
Ogni simile appetisce il suo simile.
Se tu vuoi conoscer vno, fallo parlare.
Ogni * granata nuoua spazza ben la casa.   * Broome or beesome.
Io mi sono alleuato la serpe in seno.
La discretione é la madre delle virtù.
Chi non sa fare i fatti suoi, peggio fá quei d'altri.
L'auaro non fa mai miglior opera, che quando tira le calze.
Costui mi riesce meglio à pane ch' à farina.
Fá come il can pauroso, che tira la coda fra le gambe.
Non crede al santo se non fá miracolo.
Egli há troppo buon vino á si cattiua * botte.   * A Butte, or hoggeshead.
Se l'é rosa, la fiorira.
Quando la Pera é matura, conuien che la caggia.
Quando il villan é solo sopra il fico,
Non há parente alcun, ne buon amico.
Chi há fiel in bocca, non può sputar mele.
E difficilissimo andar á veder macinare, senza imbiancarsi (di farina.
Ogni vn chiama la gatta gatta.
Il pazzo fá meglio i fatti suoi, ch' il sauio quelli d'altri.
Gli adulatori si lasciano pigliare al boccone come pesce.

L

Non v'è maggior male che l'ignoranza.
La gola, il sonno, & l'otiose piume,
Hanno del mondo ogni virtù sbandita.
E bruttissima cosa tollerar un huomo malitioso che ponga la bocca in cielo.
Sempre dopo la gloria ne vien l'inuidia.
Dio voglia che quel oro non riesca Orpello.
Tutt' il nostro proceder non è altro ch'un aggirarsi intorno, come una * farfalla intorno al lume.

*A Gnatte.

Chi così vuol, così habbia.

*Skrape. Il gallo canta con buona voce, ma non resta à * raspar con le vnghie.

Par ch'egli habbia questa ventura di cascar in piedi come le gatte.

Si và per più strade, à Roma.

* A Snare. Si tende vn * laccio alle lepri, vna *ragna à gli Vccelli, vna Rete à pesci, & à gli huomini si tendono l'Insidie.

* A fowlinge Nette. Chi non può pigliar vccelli, mangi la * ciuetta.

Non si và alla fama sott' il coltrone, ne co'l dormire su la coltrice, & chi dorme in questo modo lascia di se vn fumo in aria, & vna schiuma nell'acqua.

O bene ò male tutt' è faua.

* An Owle. Chi nõ sà adulare nõ sà conuersare: ma si dice meglio che.

L'adulatore è amico nel conuersare con parole & inimico nel animo co' fatti.

Vi corre ancor vn altro Prouerbio più volgare che lodeuole che.

Chi non sa dissimulare non sa viuere.

La fortuna non sà sedere: Colui è degno d'ogni male, che della sua fortuna si vergogna. Dicono gli ignoranti ventura Dio, poco senno basta: Et vorrei buona Fortuna, la sapienza chi la vuol la tolga: Chi non ha ventura non vadi à pescare.

Tanto

VOLGARI.

Tanto è del auaro quel che poſsiede, quanto quel che non poſ-
ſiede.
Sempre pioue, quando io fó bucato.
Come iò vò in Chieſa, mi cade il Campanile in capo. *Detto d'Homero diuentato Prouerbio.*
Amico fin ál Altare.
Anche gli ſtolti conoſcono la coſa poi ch'ella è fatta.
Gli huomini grandi hanno à morire in piedi. *Prouerbi tratti dalle Hiſtorie.*
Il Romano vince ſedendo.
Egli hà fatto il figliuol Prodigo. *Prouerbi cauati da' ſacri libri.*
Egli è venuto ſenza la veſte nuptiale.
Non ſi cognoſce Errore, la doue regna Amore. *Prouerbi fatti per vna Getildònna Saneſe.*
Chi vuol ſaluar honore, ſdegno in fronte, & fuoco in cuore.
Doue non è la ſperanza del bene, non è la paura del male.
Il pianger i morti nõ rileua, & la vendetta sfoga l'odio aſſai.
Se il lagrimar ne medicaſſe il male,
Et piangendo il dolor finiſſe,
Per le lagrime ogni vn darebbe l'oro.
  Chi oſſerua queſte tre coſe non haurà mai conteſa aucuna.
Cedere al maggiore, perſuadere con modeſtia al minore, & conſentire al vguale.
Ad amor paleſe rare volte ò non mai è conceduto felice fine. *Del Boccacio.*
Fauciulla à tempo non maritata, ſpeſſo ſi marita ſuerginata.
Tien la fortuna mentre che tu l'hai,
  Che ſi ti eſce di man mai più l'haurai.
La Zingara ad altrui la ſorte dice,
  Et la ſua non conoſce l'infelice.
Aſpettare, & non venire, ſeruire & non aggradire,
  Star in letto & non dormire, ſono tre coſe da morire.
Il miſer ſuole dar facil credenza à quel che vuole.
Sempre che l'inimico è più poſſente,
Più chi perde accettabile ha la ſcuſa.
Ambaſciator pena non porta.

L ij

Del Ariosto. *L'huomo nè per star, nè per fuggire,*
Al suo fisso destin può contradire.
Perch' il porro ha il capo bianco, la coda è verde.
Le cose quantunque molto piacciono, hauendone soperchia
 copia rincrescono.
Del Ariosto. *Ogn' vn corre à far legna,*
Al arbore, ch' il vento in terra getta.
Del Cortegiano. *La facilità non impedisce l'elegantia.*
La compagnia nel male suol allegierir il male.
I giouani hanno copia di tempo, i vecchi n'han carestia.
Ama, & sarai amato.
*Di Platone. * *L'amar altrui è il vero prezzo con che si compra Amore.*
I diauoli non sono sì negri come si depingono.
L'arbore che di continuo si trapianta non fà mai frutto.
Vfficio pregato è mezzo pagato.
Di nouello ogni cosa è bella.
Milano la grande, Venetia la ricca, Genoua la superba,
 Fiorenza la bella, Napoli la gentile.
Prouerbio Napolitano. *Balsant di quatro, ò vendre, ò barratre: Balsant di tre canal*
 di Re: Balsant d'vno, non dar anniffuno,
Di tre cose il Fiorentino ne fa vna frulla,
A Dio, mi raccommando, vuoi tu nulla.
Del Petrarcha. *Piaga antiueduta assai men duole.*
E meglio hauer vn buon porco, ch' vna bella tosa.
Non stuzzicar il can che dorme.
Dall' vnghie si conosce il Leone.
Chi muore in campo, muore in letto d'honore.
Non si ponno coglier le rose senza punger le mani.

Motti brieui ch'hanno del Prouerbio.

* The forename vsed to be giuen to a Nunne. *Costui ha del sale in zucca: cio è egl' è molto ingenioso.*
Donna * monna Zucca al vento: cio è di poco ceruello.
Piaccia a Dio che la mia Zucca mandi fuori il suo seme.

VOLGARI.

Io caualco alla * *stradiotta, pochi arnesi mi fanno.* * A light
Ha tanti libri di lettere in capo ch' vn Asino ne sarebbe ca- horse man.
La tua opera anderà in monte.   (*rico.*
Ma vegniamo a meza lama: Gli dette vna buona * *picchia-* * Knoke.
  ta: Saltò di * *Palo in* * *frasca.* * Stake.
                                                   * A bough of
Gli ho dato con la sferza vn buon cauallo.   a tree.
Ho serbato vn colpo maestro.
I poueri * *capessoni han fatto il pane.*   * Great
Egl' ha posto il tetto.   Succia su quello.   heddes.
Dice le cose si alte che non si puo pigliar la * *mira.*
De gli incorrigibili si dè mandar le radice al sole. * The sight.
Se voi vi lasciate l'ossa, vostro danno: La malitia ha fatte
  profondissime radici: Sò che tu l'hai hauuta buona á ca-
  pello: Gli ignoranti sono pur cresciuti senza * *inaffarli.* * To water
Come ha tocco due volte in capo di messer Eccellente, egli
  gomfia, come vna * *botta.   Si vantaua d'amazzar l'aria:* * A Toade.
Star non si può a petto con lui: Dar la stretta ad vno.
Hebbe nome mezzo forfante, mezzo mariuolo, il reste poi
  era tutto poltrone.
Vn certo mercantuzzo di stringhe: Vn Asinaccio da bastone:
  Vn bestionacchio sperticato da venderlo à canne come i
  campi, ò à farui presente á vn lungo remo: Vn Asinac-
  cio pezzo d'huomo: Vn bestiuolo da poco ceruello.
Lo darà il Boia bello, & fritto al diauolo: Lo dò alle forche:
  Mi ritirai con questo cocomero nel capo alla villa.
S'è cauata la maschera.
Non pensate ch'io vccelli á presenti: Vn huomo alquanto
  di sale. Heueua il piede in due staffe: cio è si poteua
  ò bene ò male interpretar i fatti ò i detti suoi.
Gl' hauete tolto quello á torto, che non gli potete rendere
  á ragione, cio è la vita: *Chi così vuol, così habbia:*
Io ti darò tanti, & tanti, ch' io ti cauerò il * *ruzzo del capo.* * Skoffinge,
Non me ne sò né grado, né gratia.   or iestinge.

L iij

Pare che quella cosa cerchi il suo centro.
Poi alla fine sono iti à monte con gli altri.
Gl' è terreno da piantar carotte: Ha l'ali più grandi ch' il nido: Più sù sta mona Luna: Dà del buon per la pace: Hà la fede Greca, cio è egl'è disleale: *Dorme con gli occhi aperti: A lui si cangiò il pelo: Che si dè far dunque? Stringer le spalle: Dare il* crollo alla bilancia: *Colui fu il primo che ruppe il ghiaccio: Gli s'è portato il cappello rosso,* cio è ha hauuto la buona nuoua: *Ha vnto le mani al giudice: Ha cattiui vicini: M'ha dato à credere* lucciole per lanterne: *Costui braua à credenza: Ho dato nello scartato: Hà preso vn granchio: ha mangiato vn' osso: voi empiete la valigia come vn zoccolante* à scrocco. *Dormite al par d'el piumaccio: Ei suda di bel Gennaio: Hà pisciato in più neue: Io ho reso l'arme à San Giorgio: Si messe in dozzena con le stringhe rotte. Sono saui à credenza, & matti á contanti. Di tal moneta l'hauete pagato, quali erano state le derrate vendute. Tu che non hai ancora rasciuti gl'occhi. Egli haueua à buona* cauiglia legato l'Asino: *A madonna poco fila gli si tringuano i* cintolini. *Costei sente del scemo. E terreno da' ferri miei.* Star con le Muse in Parnaso, fare fascio d'ogni herba.

Amici di proferta assai si truoua
Ancor chi stanno con la borsa aperta,
Quando si vien al fatto della pruoua,
Borsa serrata, amici non si truoua.
Chi dà tosto, dà due volte.
La gratia presta si radoppia, & la tarda suanisce.
Le gratie non aspettate, soglion esser più grate.
Ma non si può sforzare il Popone.
In fine in fine i quai col pane sono buoni, & ogni cosa hà il suo rimedio, fuor che la morte.

Ouerwaight, or the shaking.

* Gloowe wormes.

* Without paying any thing.

* A ringe in a wall.
The garters.

La morte anchora dà minor pena, che l'indugio della morte.
E molto meglio tosto morire, che viuendo languire.
La morte di se stessa non è misera, ma la via che conduce
　àla morte è misera.
E meglio ritornar in dietrò, che andar errando inanzi.
Meglio è goderfi il poco, ch' il bramar assai con trauaglio.
L'huomo risoluto non depende dalle cose a venire: l'aspetta,
　si bene: & gode (il meglio ch' egli può) le cose
　　presenti : Del Autore.

Se non contento, almen risoluto.
C. M.